The BEAD BOOK

A Step-by-Step Guide to the Creative Art of Beading

VICTORIA DUTTON

with special photography by
GARTH BLORE

LEOPARD

This edition published 1996 by Leopard,
an imprint of Random House UK Ltd,
20 Vauxhall Bridge Road,
London SW1V 2SA

This book was designed and produced by Todtri Productions Limited
P.O. Box 572, New York, NY 10116-0572 FAX: (212) 279-1241

Printed and bound in Singapore

ISBN 0 7529 0440 X

Author: Victoria Dutton

Publisher: Robert M. Tod
Designer and Art Director: Ron Pickless
Editor: Nicolas Wright
Typeset and DTP: Blanc Verso/UK

CONTENTS

Introduction

Beads and bead work seem to be more popular than ever. Whether the initial interest is aroused by a desire to re-string an old favorite, such as a necklace that has been hidden away in the back of a jewelry box, or to design and make a completely new matching set of necklace, bracelet and earrings, the opportunities for producing beautiful pieces have never been greater. More and more craft shops and haberdashery stores are stocking threads, findings and, increasingly, beads, while specialist bead shops are springing up all over the place, and if you turn to the back pages of most craft-based magazines and journals, you will find dozens of advertisements for obtaining every possible kind of bead and bead-related item by mail order.

Opposite: Even the simplest of combinations, such as this twist of strands of bugles, looks fresh and appealing – and when you get tired of it, you can always snip through the threads and reuse the beads.

Below: Little specialized equipment is needed to get started with beading. You will soon find that the only constraints on your work are those imposed by time.

Beads are such beautiful objects that it seems a shame to hide them away. However, as your stocks increase and you find yourself buying beads and rescuing broken necklaces from jumble sales and charity (thrift) shops, you will have to find a way to organize your collection. If you have the space, glass containers allow you the best of both worlds – you can organize and admire your beads at the same time. When space is limited, compartmentalized boxes like these are ideal.

It is not difficult to find the reasons for this interest. Beads are inherently beautiful things, and simply possessing a string of antique beads or coming across some of the beautiful glass and ceramic beads that are becoming increasingly available is enough to spark a fascination for these lovely objects.

Beading is one of the few crafts that requires scarcely any specialist equipment, yet it can produce uniquely beautiful and wearable objects. With just some thread, a needle or two and good light, combined with a little patience and practice, it is possible to create stunning pieces of jewelry. You will be able to re-string broken necklaces or reuse beads from old-fashioned pieces that you find in second-hand shops and even at jumble sales.

A single pair of pliers and a little practice at turning loops and clipping wire to length will quickly enable you to produce earrings to match the necklaces and bracelets you make and to embellish chokers with wired drops.

Whether you use beads for your own satisfaction and enjoyment, whether you want to make unusual and personal gifts for your friends and family, or whether you want to develop your hobby into a profitable pastime, the opportunities for expressing your creative talents and for producing beautiful and wearable items are virtually limitless. The only danger is that you may find that searching for unusual and lovely beads takes more and more of your time, as you comb through secondhand-shops and market stalls.

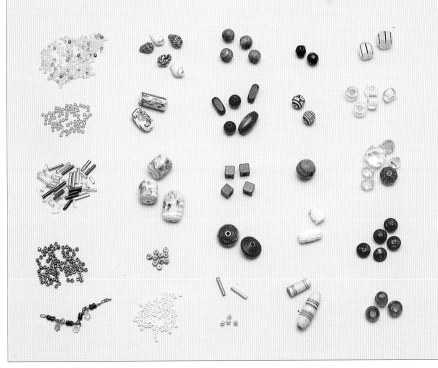

Above: Combining different textures can produce wonderfully subtle designs, especially when the colors selected harmonize closely. Matt beads will make glass seem to shine and sparkle more brightly, while metallized beads will reflect and enhance the colors of their neighbors.

Left: Beads have been made from the earliest times and some of the most desirable beads are semi-precious stones and beautifully worked glass, but today's bead enthusiast is more likely to use ordinary glass, ceramic, wood and plastic beads, and there is such a variety to choose from that it can be difficult to know what to use.

CHAPTER ONE
TYPES OF BEAD

TYPES OF BEAD

CONVERSION CHART
The sizes are approximate and
should be used as a guide only.

mm	in
3	1/8
6	1/4
10	3/8
13	1/2
16	5/8
19	3/4
22	7/8
25	1

As bead work has increased in popularity, specialist bead shops have sprung up in towns across Europe and North America. These are the ideal place to buy beads, especially if you are working on a fairly limited range of pieces, because you are able to have a close look at, and sometimes handle, the beads before you buy them, which not only gives you an opportunity to check that there are no flaws in the beads and that the holes are smooth and centrally placed, but also allows you to consider whether they will combine happily with the other beads in your planned design. Inevitably, though, seeing such a large range of beads will encourage you to buy other beads and inspire you to create new pieces, so be warned!

Beads are also available in craft shops, haberdashery stores and department stores, and you can occasionally find just what you are looking for, although the choice is more limited than in a shop that supplies nothing but beads and bead-related items. Nevertheless, you can see the beads at close quarters and judge how they will look when they are used in your designs. However, you are likely to find a much wider range if you look through the catalogues of mail-order suppliers, many of which include color illustrations. Even though you have to wait for your order to be delivered and it is sometimes difficult to assess color and texture from a photograph, mail order, especially when you become hooked on bead work, is the most economical and, if you do not live near a large town, certainly the most convenient way of buying beads.

BEAD SIZES

Beads sizes are given in millimetres (mm) even in the United States. The measurement is usually the diameter of the bead – that is, the distance through the hole. The most often used beads range in size from 2mm to 18mm, although larger ones are, of course, available and can be used. Some beads are measured by diameter times length – 4 x 10mm, for example. Circular cabochons are also sold by the diameter, while the size of oval stones is indicated by the width x height at the widest points – for example, 8 x 6mm or 18 x 13mm.

Thus, if you were planning a necklace approximately 16in (40cm) long, you would need about 100 4mm beads and about 40 10mm beads.

A choker is normally about 14in (35.5cm) long, while the type of necklace sometimes called a "princess" is 16–18in (40–46cm) and a "matinee" necklace is 20–24in (51–61cm) long. On average, bracelets should be 6–7in (15–18cm) long. However, pieces can always be made longer or shorter to suit the wearer.

Opposite: Venice has been famous for the production of glass since the late Middle Ages, and many beautiful glass beads were and are made at the Murano works.

There are so many kinds of glass beads that it would be possible to use nothing else to produce an almost limitless variety of earrings, necklaces and bracelets. Whether you are using ordinary opaque rocailles or the darkest blue ovals, combine them to create the effect you want – dark blue and gold looks sophisticated, sky blue and sunny yellow look fresh and cheerful.

GLASS BEADS

Glass is one of the most versatile and one of the most often used materials in bead making. The material seems first to have been used to make beads in ancient Egypt and in ancient Rome, and it has also been used for centuries in India. In Europe, the glassworks at Murano, Venice, developed into a major center of glass making during the Renaissance, and Venetian glass beads are still highly desirable. Most glass beads are molded, but blown glass beads are still made in Venice and decorated with flecks of gold. Such beads are expensive, but if you can afford only one or two, use them to form the centerpiece of a design that will show these wonderful beads off to greatest effect.

Lamp beads are made by winding molten glass around copper wire, which is heated over a lamp – hence the name. The bead is decorated with "goldstone", which is a type of glass containing metal dust that originated in Venice, and they are usually finished with raised eye and trim decorations of the kind that can be seen on beads made in ancient Rome and Egypt. Lamp beads are traditionally made in India, but they also come

from Italy, central Europe, including the Czech Republic, and Italy. The lamp beads made in Bohemia are particularly lustrous.

The word "millefiori" will be familiar to anyone who has ever admired the paperweights that use this technique. Millefiori beads, while not having the butterflies and flowers found in the paperweights, are amazingly intricate, and are formed from long canes of colored glass, drawn out to incredible fineness and then fused together.

A special group of glass beads are known as "trade beads" – they were used for barter when European traders first began to do business in Africa, and boatloads of beads are said to have been taken there.

Glass is also used to make faceted beads. These days you are more likely to find and use molded beads, but hand-cut beads, although expensive, can still be found. They have a magical sparkle and sheen.

Glass is also used to make rocailles and bugles, the little round beads and tubes that no bead worker can be without. Both are made from long tubes of glass, which are stretched and cut to size. Rocailles, which are sometimes called seed beads or pound beads, are roundish and are

Lamp beads are available in a variety of shapes, including drops, cylinders and ovals, as well as these pretty round ones, which came from India.

Overleaf: The variety of glass beads that can be bought easily and inexpensively makes it almost impossible not to want to begin immediately to create something beautiful with them. It is not difficult to understand why some people become obsessed with beads.

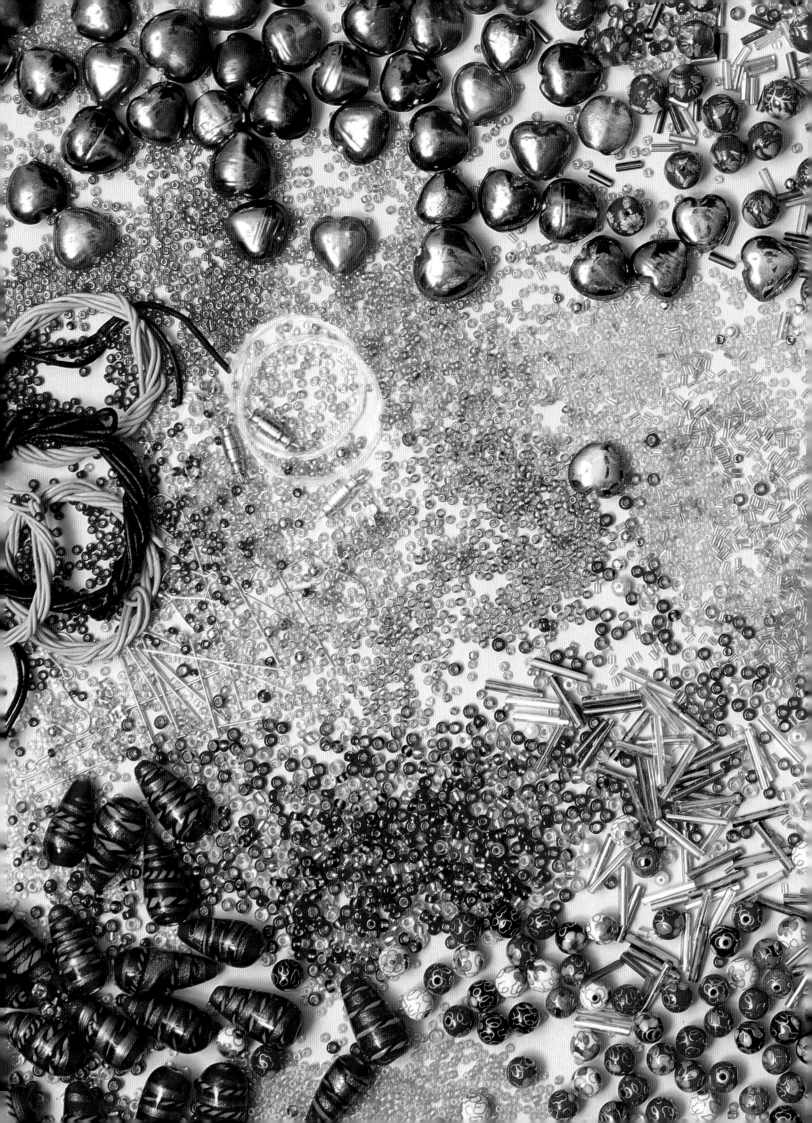

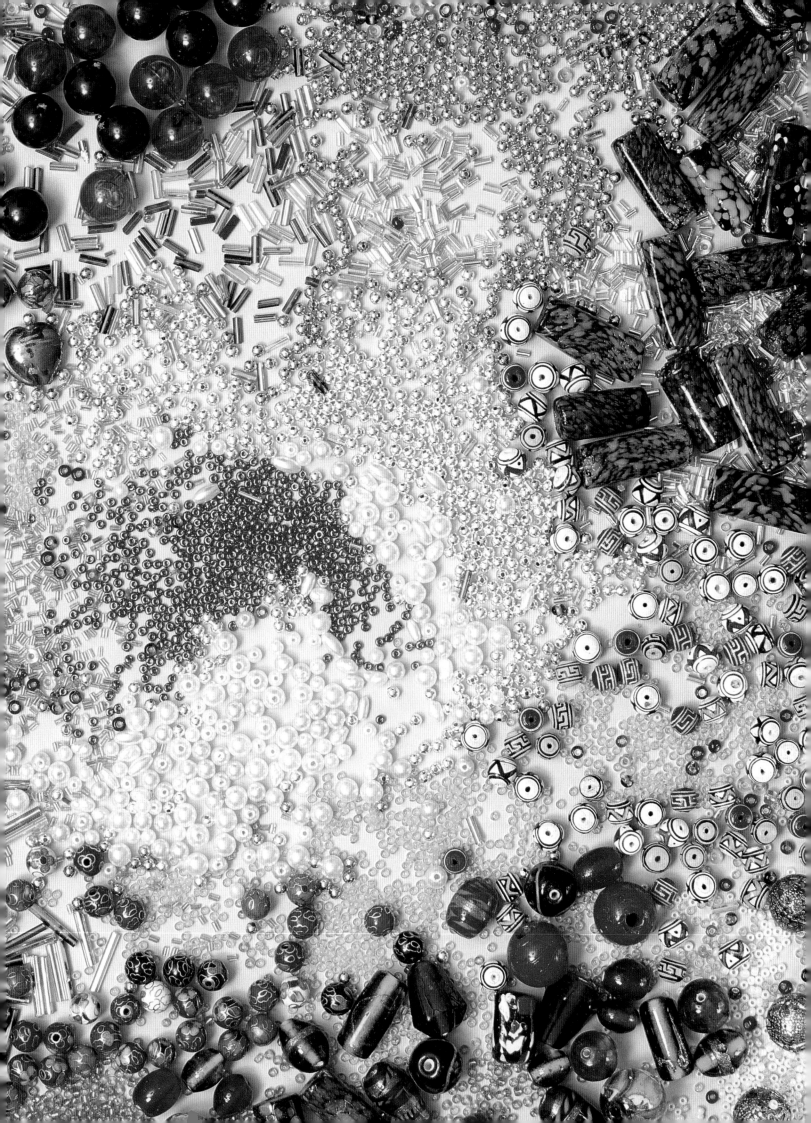

available in five sizes. Bugles are little tubes and are found in four sizes. Both are available in a variety of finishes, including opaque, silver-lined, pearlized and iridescent. The tiniest rocailles are used in embroidery, and opaque rocailles are ideal for loomwork. Larger rocailles are often used as spacers between larger beads. Bugles can be used as spacers, in brickstitch and in embroidery. They are also useful in drops for earrings.

Bugles and rocailles are made in the same colors and finishes, so it is possible to combine them in the same piece for some stunning effects. However, if you are considering using rocailles as spacers in a special piece, it is worth examining them carefully and even roughly stringing all the beads before you begin so that you can discard those rocailles that are unevenly formed and those that do not have holes exactly in the center.

Glass beads can be as large or as small as you wish. Long strands of small, bright, opaque beads can be made into simple but effective necklaces, while large, single discs make striking pendants.

Opposite: Rocailles used to be sold by length, in strands, but today you are more likely to buy small packets by weight. Their slight irregularities – holes are often off-center and shapes vary – are part of the charm.

Ceramic was probably one of the first materials to be used for beads, and the hand-painted examples from Peru (on the right) are decorated in traditional patterns and colors, the warm terracotta being especially attractive.

CERAMIC BEADS

Clay and dried mud must have been among man's earliest means of adornment, and ceramic beads are still being made – for example, plain ceramic beads are made in the UK, and these are found in unusual shapes, as well as perfect spheres.

Among the most appealing of ceramic beads are Peruvian clay beads, which come in a variety of sizes, shapes and hole sizes. The drops are ideal for earrings, but they are also available as cylinders and spheres. They are basically white with red, green and blue hand-painted geometric or pictorial decorations.

Blue and white ceramic beads from China recall the blue and white willow-pattern, but some painted porcelain beads from China are decorated with beautiful flowers, dragons and birds. Some ceramic beads from Greece are decorated with transfer patterns, and they are made with a variety of finishes, including luster and glaze.

Semi-precious Materials

Precious stones are, of course, of little relevance to the home bead worker, but semi-precious stones - gemstones – are a different matter.

Amethyst, agate, turquoise, howlite (which is often dyed), blank onyx, malachite, jade, hematite, quartz, garnet tiger's eye, obsidian ... the list is almost endless. Most are available as round beads in sizes 4mm, 6mm and 8mm, and they are also sometimes sold as drops and also as cabochons. Look out for chips, which are supplied ready drilled and can be strung to make pretty necklaces.

Amber is not a stone; it is the fossilized resin of a type of pine tree and it occurs natural in the Baltic, Sicily and in parts of South America. It can be transparent or opaque, and the colors range from yellow, through greenish-brown and orange to deep, rich brown. Amber is comparatively light and somewhat warm to the touch. Although it was called *elektron* by the Greeks, rubbing a bead to see if it gives off a slight electric charge is not a

Above: Real amber, as seen on the left, is very expensive and quite rare. However, beads made from amber-colored plastic or a pressed resin can look just as good.

Opposite: If you have a hobby drill, it is possible to drill holes in individual gemstones and to string them. It is, however, just as easy – and a lot less time-consuming – to buy pre-drilled stones. You can obtain mixed gemstones, which can be used to make a very attractive necklace, or packets of a single type – undyed howlite and amethysts are shown here.

reliable means of identifying amber, because many plastics also give a slight electric charge. The material called "ambroid" is made from melted-down chips of amber; it is not as breakable as the real thing and has visible strata.

Jet is fossilized coal, and jet beads were very popular in Victorian Britain, where mourning was a way of life. Ebony and "bog oak" are sometimes mistaken for jet, although the grain in the wood is nearly always visible, and most small black faceted beads are glass.

WOOD, BONE AND SHELL BEADS

Bone and horn are traditional materials for beads, although more likely to be encountered these days in necklaces found in antique shops and second-hand stores. Trade in ivory is, of course, now thankfully illegal. Wood, however, is used for beads of every possible size, shape, weight and color. It can be simply shaped, intricately carved, dyed, painted and varnished. Sometimes the natural color and grain are allowed to show through; sometimes the wood is decorated with bands of inlaid brass. Many wooden beads from the Philippines are made from plantation-grown timber, and coco beads, which are light and often brightly colored, are made from the husk of coconuts.

Shells and shell-discs were used as money in Africa, India, Polynesia and North America until fairly recent times, and cowry shells are often seen strung together.

Real pearls, which are produced by the pearl oyster, are rare and lovely, and a carefully calibrated stranded necklace is still one of the most desirable of all items of jewelry. Freshwater pearls, which vary in size and color,

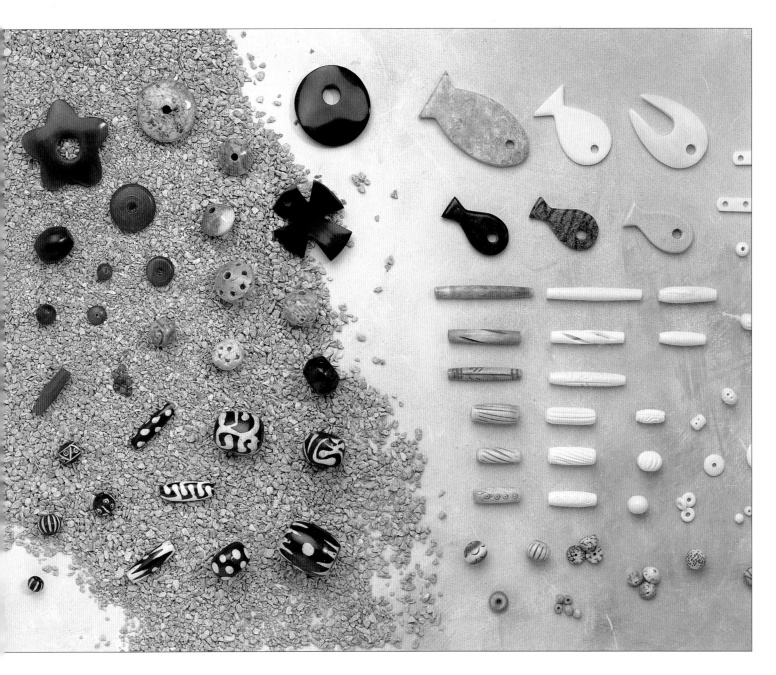

Above: Horn, bone and stone have been worked into ornaments for as long as man has had the tools to fashion them. These days, the bones used for such beads as the spirals shown center right are from cattle, bleached to make them brilliant white. Horn beads, as shown at top left, are naturally quite dark, almost black, but they, too, are often bleached and then dyed.

Opposite: The natural colors of bone and stone combine beautifully together in these examples.

Previous page: Wooden beads are ideal for children to work with, especially when they can be strung on cord or leather.

come from the pearl mussel. Imitation pearls, which are available in a range of pretty pastel colors, are made either of plastic with a pearlized coating or, more successfully, from pearlized glass.

Mother-of-pearl, or nacre, which comes from the innermost layer of shells, both seashells and snail shells, has been used in the Far East for centuries for inlaid work and for carving. In the West it is, perhaps, most often seen when it is used for buttons, but it is also occasionally used for inlaying and it is possible to obtain all kinds of pretty shapes in mother-of-pearl that you can incorporate in your jewelry designs. The delicate iridescent colors are the result of the way in which light is reflected from the thin, chalky scales, of lamellae, of the shell.

Mother-of-pearl is usually available in two main forms – the white shell, which is usually supplied in polished, pre-cut shapes, and the colored form, or abalone, which can also be bought in pre-cut shapes but that also available in pieces. If you need to join two pieces of abalone or mother-of-

pearl together, slightly roughen the areas that will be glued with a piece of fine sandpaper before applying the adhesive. This is the easiest way of decorating items such as hair slides or large brooch pins. Remember to leave the adhesive to dry for 10–12 hours before wearing the piece.

METAL BEADS

Silver and silver-colored beads from India and the Far East are available in a huge variety of sizes, shapes and patterns, and Indian jewelry often features beautifully crafted filigree beads, which are often combined with precious and semi-precious stones. In North Africa there is a long tradition of working with silver to produce beautiful filigree beads and delicately

Opposite: Wooden beads are available in a surprising range of colors and shapes. You can even find striped beads, made from slices of woods, such as redwood, kamagong and bayong, laminated together.

Below: Metal beads with "gold" or "silver" finishes often look best when they are combined with glass beads or gemstones. Use them to introduce contrasts of color, shape and texture.

engraved pendants. Look our for beads that are made from recycled materials – including saucepans and even bits of old automobiles – which are made in parts of Africa.

Many apparently metal beads, however, are formed on a resin or plastic core, thinly coated with a metal finish. The finish rubs away over time, as beads chafe against each other.

PLASTIC BEADS

These days plastic is used to simulate practically every kind of material, and many plastic beads are so convincing that it is hardly worth spending a lot on the real thing. Beads that look like pearl, bone, horn and wood can be used in all those pieces where the genuine material is not obtainable – ivory, for example, unless it is antique, is no longer available. Many apparently metal beads are, in fact, plastic, and they can be distinguished from the genuine article only by weight.

Perhaps the best plastic beads are those that do not pretend to be anything but plastic, and the material really comes into its own when it is molded into all kinds of shapes, both geometric and natural. Flowers, leaves and even fruit can used in drop earrings or combined with faux pearls and glass beads to make very pretty necklaces. Cones, discs and drops exploit plastic's best characteristics.

Opposite: "Silver" beads en masse can look less than sophisticated. Combined with plain crystal or black beads, however, they immediately become stylish and elegant.

Below: Combine pretty pastel shades of plastic and glass beads for summery accessories. Softly shimmering "pearls" can be made into delicate single-strand necklaces or drop earrings. The flowery cylinders are decal beads from Greece – that is, the motif is applied as a transfer to the hand-rolled ceramic bead. The speckled glass beads – sometimes called Picasso beads – look lovely on their own or when they are used with bugles and rocailles.

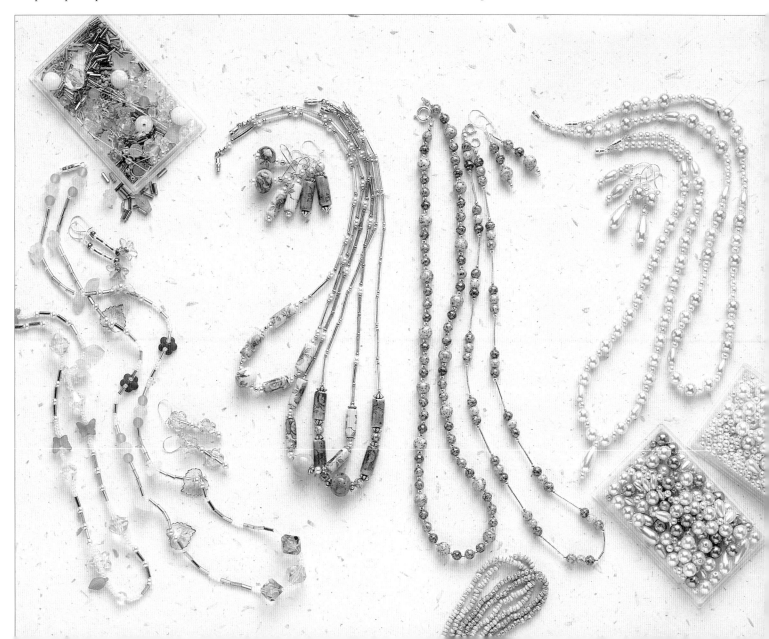

It is possible to obtain beads that have been "antiqued" so that they appear to have the patina of age. These beads are, in fact, plastic, not, metal, and they are, therefore, very light. Use them with discretion.

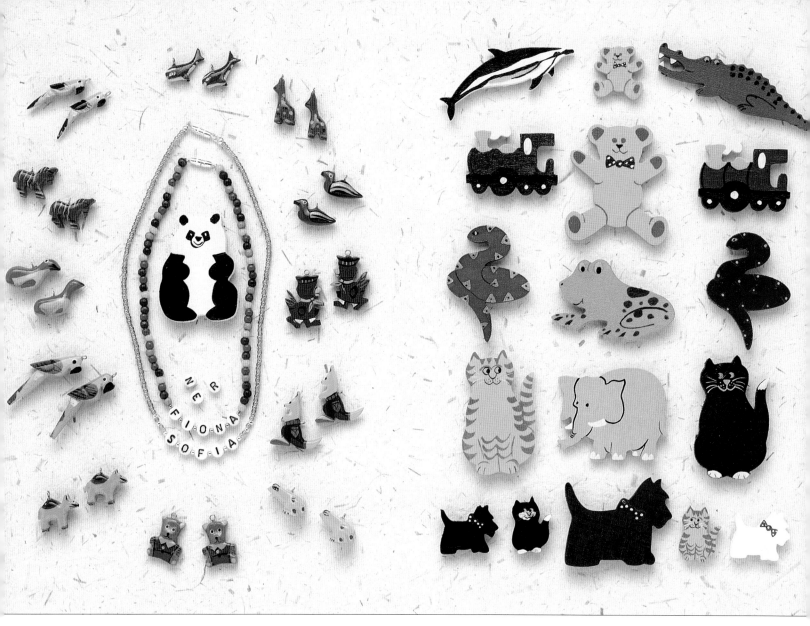

Above: Painted wooden beads can be used for earrings – look out for ones that have little hooks in the top – or they can be used to hang on loops or, with a brooch back, as a simple brooch.

Right: It is hardly fair to classify these brilliantly colored beads as novelty items. The millefiore beads (top left) are beautiful examples of the Venetian craft of transforming glass canes into almost unbelievable designs, while the Peruvian ceramic beads are hand painted in traditional designs and colors. The wonderful birds and fish, however, which were made in Guatemala are true novelties – unusual and inspirational.

NOVELTY BEADS

Usually made of plastic or wood, there is an enormous group of beads that are just for fun – use them for bizarre earring drops or in a fantasy necklace. Children will love playing with beads that feature their favorite animals or that can spell out their names.

MAKING YOUR OWN BEADS

Most handicraft shops and toy shops stock modeling clay, which can be either of the oven-bake or air-dried kind. This is the perfect medium for making beads and pendants. Before you start, knead the clay for about 10 minutes to make it malleable (if you are working in a cold room it may take a little longer). Roll it out on a clean, flat surface to make sheets from which you can cut all manner of shapes, including leaves, petals and even tiny animal shapes. You can also make little millefiori slices, which can be pressed to the sides of balls of clay. There are several excellent books available that are packed with ideas and advice on using the different makes of clay to produce some quite amazing results.

Papier mâché is a versatile material. These brightly painted beads were made from paper pulp and decorated with acrylic paints.

Begin your experiments with single colors – remember that different colors can be easily combined to create new, subtle shades – and pattern the surface of the shapes by pressing on pieces of fabric with different textures, such as netting or lace. Use the barrel of an old ball-point pen to make a pattern or circles or cover the surface of the clay with the small indentations made by an old nailbrush or toothbrush. The point of a cocktail stick can be used to indent lines and veins on leaf shapes or simply to create abstract swirls and curves. When you feel confident with using a single color, experiment with marbelized and millefiori patterns.

For some time, too, it has been possible to buy metallic powders to give a gold or silver finish to the clay, and the manufacturers of all the main kinds of clay have steadily increased the range of powders that can be brushed on the surface of the clay to create all kinds of interesting effects. Bronze, for example, looks especially pretty with mother-of-pearl, and one of the easiest ways of making a brooch is to fill a brooch blank with clay – black is probably the best color to choose – and then to insert pieces of abalone in the clay. When you are happy with the arrangement, use a fine, soft paintbrush to apply the powder, then bake the clay in the normal way. When the clay has been baked and is cool, remove the abalone and glue it in place, then brush over the whole surface with one of the proprietary varnishes, either matt or gloss, to fix the powder.

Chapter Two

Findings, Materials & Equipment

ℱINDINGS, ℳATERIALS & ℰQUIPMENT

Opposite: The basic equipment needed to begin working with beads is very simple. At first, probably the only items you will need to buy especially will be a good pair of pliers and, probably, a pair of metal snips. Shown here is a selection, including wire cutters, round-nosed pliers and snipe-nosed pliers. You will also need beading needles and some small, sharp sewing scissors. Remember to choose a thread that is suitable for the beads you are using. Seen here, from the top, is a piece of fine wire used in place of a beading needle; nylon twine, which can be used with large-holed beads; silver and gold elastic thread, which is perfect for quick bracelets and anklets; tiger tail (plastic-coated wire), which is usually finished off with calotte crimps; monofilament, which is easy to use but not suitable for lightweight beads; and linen cord, which is available in a variety of colors and looks good simply knotted before and after attractive beads.

If you do needlework or another handicraft, you will probably have many of the items you need to get started with your bead work. The threads and needles you use will, to a large extent, be determined by the kind of beads you are working with, but fine polyester thread and a small-eyed needle, together with a pair of sharp scissors are all you need to get started.

THREADS, THONGS AND CHAINS

Always use a thread that is appropriate to the beads. Precious pearls should be strung on silk, but polyester thread or nylon thread is suitable for glass while wooden or chunky ceramic beads may look better on leather or lace thong.

Polyester thread, which is available in all haberdashers, is most often used with light and medium weight beads. It is available in a variety of colors and thicknesses, so it is possible to choose a shade that is a close match to the beads you are using. When you require extra strength, the thread can be used double, but even then, the beads will hang in a smooth loop. It is also possible to obtain waxed thread, which is easy to work.

Large, heavy beads can be strung on nylon monofilament, a clear, strong gut, of the kind that you will find in angling shops. This, too, is available in a range of thicknesses and weights. Look out for the finest gauges. The gut can be used without a needle, but it is sometimes too inflexible to use with light beads, which will not hang in a smooth curve but be held in the curves in the gut.

Tiger tail, which is made of a strong metal core that is coated in clear plastic, is available in a range of thicknesses. This is the ideal thread to use with heavy beads, especially metal ones or heavy glass beads, which might cut a non-metallic thread. Like monofilament, however, it is not suitable for lightweight beads, which are not heavy enough to make it hang well.

Wooden or bone beads and large, chunky ceramic beads often look attractive when they are threaded on leather thong, which you will most often use in sizes of 1mm or 2mm. Shorter lengths of leather thong can be used to make hoop-shaped earrings. Use a large bead – metal or wood, for example – with a small bead on either side, and close the thong with a leather crimp, which can be attached by its loop to an ear fitting. chains of different gauges

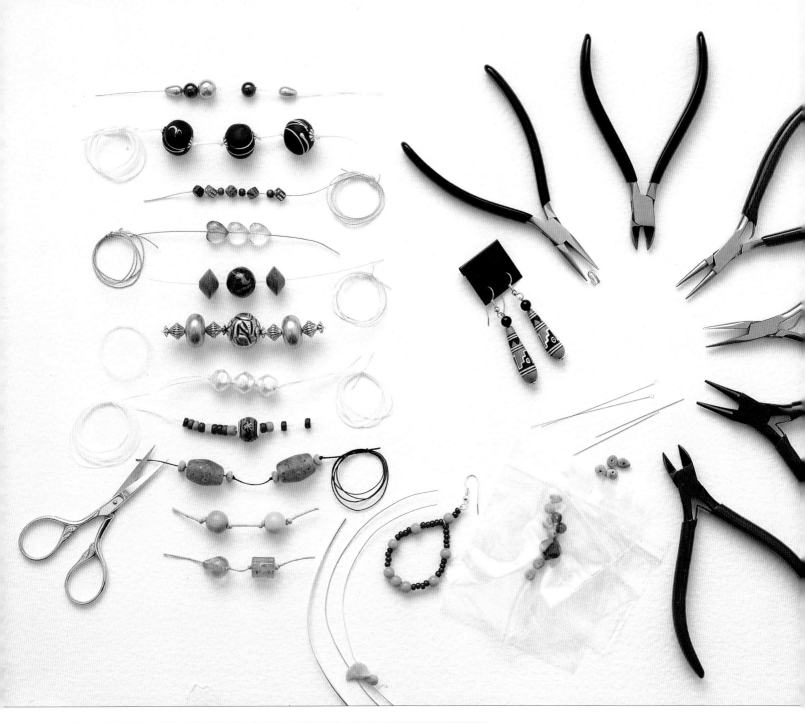

Left: The secret of successful stringing is to choose the correct thread. Silk threads are slightly more expensive, but when you are using special beads, they are worth using. Choose a color that matches your beads. Otherwise, when you are threading beads with small holes, use tiger tail, polyester thread or nylon thread. Beads with larger holes can be strung on monofilament, linen threads or even colorful silken cords. Finish off the cords with special end crimps.

sufficient to fill the ring completely – then the fastening can be pressed to close. You can add a spot of adhesive to make the closure completely secure if you wish. The decorated hoop can then be attached to the ear fitting of your choice by means of the loop in the top. Some hoops have an extra loop at the top from which an extra decoration can be suspended.

Many earrings and those necklaces and bracelets that are made from beads strung together with wire, involve the use of headpins and eyepins, Both are straight lengths of metal, which can be easily clipped to length with your pliers, onto which beads can be threaded.

Above: In addition to earring findings for pierced ears, you can obtain ear clips (bottom left) and ear screws (second row up). Also shown here are headpins and eyepins, ranging from 1in (2.5cm) to 3in (7.5cm) long. As with other findings, headpins and eyepins are available in various materials.

Left: One of the simplest kinds of earrings you can make is to thread a few beads onto a hoop, which can then be attached to a fish hook.

The difference is that headpins have a very small flattened knob at one end, while eyepins have a small loop at one end.

Simple drop earrings can be made by threading three or four beads onto a headpin. Leave about 1/4in (6mm) at the top, cutting the pin to length if necessary, then use round-nosed pliers to turn a neat loop in the top of the head pin, close to the top bead. Carefully pull back the loop so that it sits on the top of the pin, then simply slide the loop over the earring finding of your choice.

The loop at the bottom of the eyepin can be opened by using pliers to twist it sideways. A pendant-type bead or other ornament with a small loop at the top can be slipped over the loop, which can then be closed. The top of the eyepin can then be decorated with beads or simply trimmed to length, a loop formed in the top, which can then be attached to an earring finding.

Above: Cufflinks, key rings and hat and lapel pins can all be decorated with beads. The blanks are widely available in both silver and gilt finishes.

A beautifully made necklace deserves to be finished off well and used with an appropriate fastener or clasp. Bolt rings, which are used with jump rings, are the most usual means of fastening a necklace, but there are also torpedo clasps, screw clasps, spring-box clasps and trigger clasps. Calotte crimps and French crimps can be used to squeeze over knots at the end of strings of beads, and the loop in the calotte can be attached to a jump ring and thence to a clasp. Cones and tubes can be used to disguise knots at the end of strands of beads, and they are especially useful when gathered together and knot the threads of a multi-strand necklace.

Spacer bars are used in multi-strand necklaces and bracelets to separate

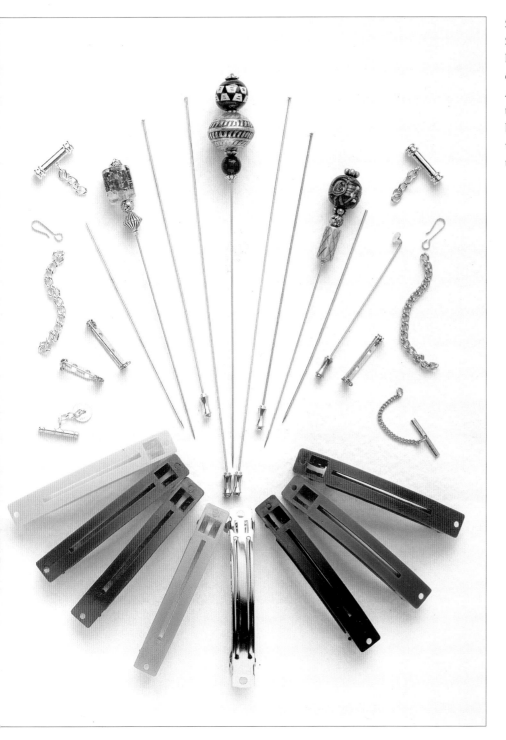

Slide blanks are easy to decorate with beads. Simply thread the beads of your choice onto the length of metal provided with the blank, which clips in place at the ends of the plastic backing. Alternatively, of course, you can simply glue them in position. Remember that metallized beads usually look best when they are combined with glass or ceramic beads – *en masse* they tend to look cheap rather than just cheerful.

the strands. Rondelles, which are sometimes inset with little crystals, are used to separate and add interest to strands of beads.

Bails, which are small pieces of wire bent into triangles, can be used for holding drop-shaped beads that have a hole in the top. Simply open out the wire and insert it in the hole in the bead. Press the sides together to hold the bead securely.

When beads and gemstones do not have holes, they can be glued into bell caps, which can then be threaded on a necklace or attached to other loops and added to earrings or chains.

Perforated discs, which are sometimes known as sieves, can be used to

Above: Among the dozens of bead-related items you can buy are tassels with integral loops, brooch backs and perforated discs or sieves.

Below: Round-nosed pliers are essential for turning neat, smooth loops. Snipe-nosed pliers, which are flattened on the inside but have round tips, can be used to open rings or close crimps.

make both clip-on earrings and brooches. The front part, which can be almost any shape you wish – circular, hexagonal, oval and so on – is covered with small holes, and this is attached by claws to the back, which can take the form of an ear clip or brooch back. The claws can either be on the front, perforated section or on the back. Use strong thread to attach beads to the front, and use glue to secure the knot before attaching the back section.

EQUIPMENT

One of the great delights of working with beads is that you can make some lovely pieces with no specialist equipment. However, as you become more interested in beads and especially if you want to use headpins and eyepins and ear fittings of various kinds, you will find it useful to have some special tools.

PLIERS

You will need a pair of round-nosed pliers for bending wire. These pliers are essential when you need to form loops to attach ear fittings, clasps and so on. Flat-nosed pliers are also useful, especially for holding findings such as jump rings when you want to bend them. Not essential but useful are side cutters, which can be used to snip headpins, eyepins and wire to length.

If you are doing a lot of bead work, you will find it helpful to have some special tweezers. Although almost any kind of tweezers will be adequate, it is possible to obtain beading tweezers, which have a circular hole in the

Use your pliers to close loops neatly when you attach your finished drops to the ear hooks.

end of one arm. The other arm has a rounded end, but it is otherwise "normal". The bead sits snugly in the hole and can be safely picked up and moved around without shooting off all over the room. Some tweezers have Teflon-coated tips so that you can safely handle real pearls and other delicate beads without fear of marking the surface.

Also available are tweezers that are specially designed to help with tying knots. These have long, tapered points to aid in pulling through thread and making sure that knots are tightened against the bead. You will also find these tweezers a boon for pulling thread and needles through the holes in beads.

SCISSORS

Small, sharp scissors are essential. Always cut thread cleanly because it otherwise tends to unravel more quickly. Keep a pair of scissors especially for needlework, because cutting paper and card is the surest way to blunt the blades, and if you use blunt scissors you will fray the thread.

If you prefer, you can use special thread clippers, which can be useful for snipping threads in awkward places. If you use tiger tail, cut it with wire cutters or snips.

NEEDLES

Some thread is stiff enough to pass through beads without a needle, and you can, if you wish, use a little adhesive to stiffen the working end of the thread. Sometimes, however, you will want or need to use a needle. You can buy flexible needles in a range of sizes. These are really nothing more than loops of wire – the loop flattens as the needle is passed through the bead. Such loop needles can be easily made from fine fuse wire: simply bend a length in half and twist the ends together to close the loop.

Rigid steel needles are also available in a range of sizes, but these have the disadvantage that the eye may not always pass easily through the holes in the beads, and the metal of the eye can chafe the thread if it is pulled through the holes too often or too energetically.

Miscellaneous

If you have a well-stocked needlework box you will probably have many of the tools and equipment you need to begin beading. There are, however, some things that you will need if and when you get bitten with the bead bug and want to make some more adventurous and unusual pieces.

Clear all-purpose adhesive can be used to secure knots. Because you only need a tiny spot of adhesive, apply the glue with the end of a wooden cocktail stick. Clear nail varnish can be used instead, and this is often more convenient, simply because you can control the amount of varnish you apply with the brush in the bottle. Protect your work surface when you use either adhesive or nail varnish.

A bead board is invaluable when you are designing necklaces. The curved groove allows you to arrange your beads just as they will appear around your neck, but at same time gives you the freedom to move them around until you are happy with the arrangement.

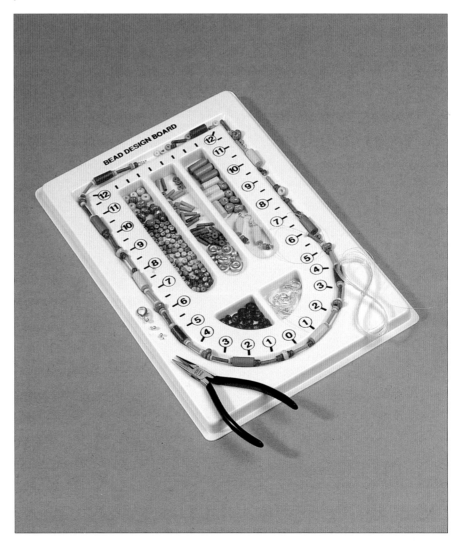

If you want to glue cabochons and gemstones to flat findings, such as ear pads or brooch pins, you will need to use a two-part epoxy adhesive. This is sold in craft and hobby shops. You may also occasionally find that you need an adhesive that will bond metal to metal, and again you should look out for epoxy resins, which are ideal for use with metal, china and glass.

A hobby drill fitted with a bit with a diameter of about 1/32in (1mm) will be useful if you have pieces of abalone that are not pre-drilled and that you would like to attach to, say, earring hoops. You might also, occasionally, wish to re-drill a bead – for example, you may want to smooth an existing hole that is so rough that it might damage the thread or you may want to increase the size of a hole so that you can incorporate the bead in a design on a thick thread. Use a regular hobby drill with wood, metal and plastic. You will need a special bit for pearls, glass, gemstones and crystal.

Although modeling clay can be used on its own to make the most amazing range of beads, you might also find it useful to keep a small amount of a neutral color for padding out the hollows in pieces of abalone or mother-of-pearl so that you can attach them more easily to a flat base. You can, of course, also embed all kinds of stones and beads in modeling clay.

You may also find that small pieces of the finest grade of sandpaper (glasspaper) or an emery board, a scalpel or craft knife and a fine-pointed paintbrush are useful.

When you begin to thread beads and to design your own earrings and necklaces you will probably find that you can manage with your beads held in the fold of a piece of paper. However, if you are planning to do a lot of designing and working with beads, you will almost certainly find that a bead board is useful. Traditional boards are simply pieces of wood with several grooves – usually about six – in the surface and, sometimes, a measuring scale along one side. The grooves enable you to position and reposition beads without their rolling about. More recently molded plastic bead boards have become available. These generally have a curved groove, often with a measuring scale alongside, and compartments in which the beads can be held while you work.

BEADING LOOM
It is possible to buy fairly inexpensive plastic beading looms, and you might want to obtain one of these if you only want to experiment or if your children want to try their hands with the process. You can also buy metal looms, which hold the threads in springs and have wooden rolls onto which the thread is wound. However, more expensive wooden ones are available, and not only do these look far nicer, they last longer and tend to be larger than the metal version.

This small beading loom is ideal for beginning your loomwork designs. Use opaque rocailles to work geometric patterns that are perfect for belts, hatbands and chokers.

CHAPTER THREE
STRINGING

ℐTRINGING

One of the easiest and most often seen ways of making a necklace or bracelet is simply by threading your beads onto a suitable thread and either attaching a clasp of some kind or even, if the necklace is long enough, knotting the thread in such a way that it can be slid under a bead and hidden from view. As the examples in this chapter will show, there is a huge variety of effects that can be achieved with this straightforward technique.

Before you begin to thread a necklace or bracelet, decide if you are going to have a symmetrical or random pattern. Are you going to repeat a combination of colors or bead shapes or are you going to make an entirely asymmetric design? Think about the overall effect you want to achieve –

The key to a successful necklace is often to limit your color palette to just one or two colors or similar tones of a color.

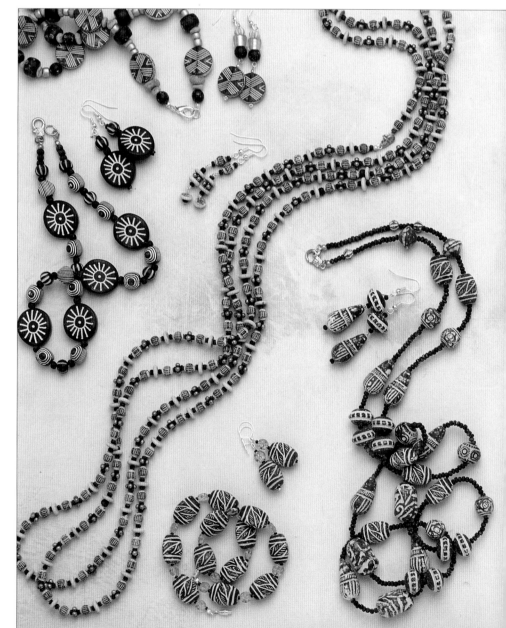

ethnic, sophisticated, amusing – and whether you are making something to accompany a particular outfit or to wear on a specific occasion. Are you making a necklace because you want to display some unusual or especially beautiful beads or are you simply making an accessory that will enhance your outfit?

If you are going to make a long necklace, without a fastener, that can be slipped over the head and worn doubled, a carefully thought-out symmetrical pattern might not be appropriate and is unlikely, in any case, to be seen for what it is. A shorter, single-strand necklace with a clasp, on the other hand, may call for carefully arranged beads in descending order of size, with each side a mirror image of the other, or it may demand that larger beads be balanced by smaller ones or a group of a more dominant color. Even wholly random patterns are not just strings of beads plucked from your collection, however. Some colors, textures and shapes go better together than others. Bear in mind, too, that heavy beads should not generally be used next to light, delicate ones. Apart from the fact that the necklace will not hang smoothly, the delicate beads could easily be damaged.

Think, too, about the practical aspects of any design. Ask yourself if the necklace is going to be worn by someone who is tall and dark or someone who might be short and fair? The length of the finished piece should be appropriate for the wearer.

Overleaf left: Even rather ordinary strands of a single color can be made more interesting by the use of different shapes and sizes.

Overleaf right: Wooden beads are available in an almost bewildering range of sizes and colors – among the woods represented here are maple, willow, cedar and tilia (lime). The neutral colors of these beads harmonize well together, and the simple stringing techniques are well suited to these natural materials.

53

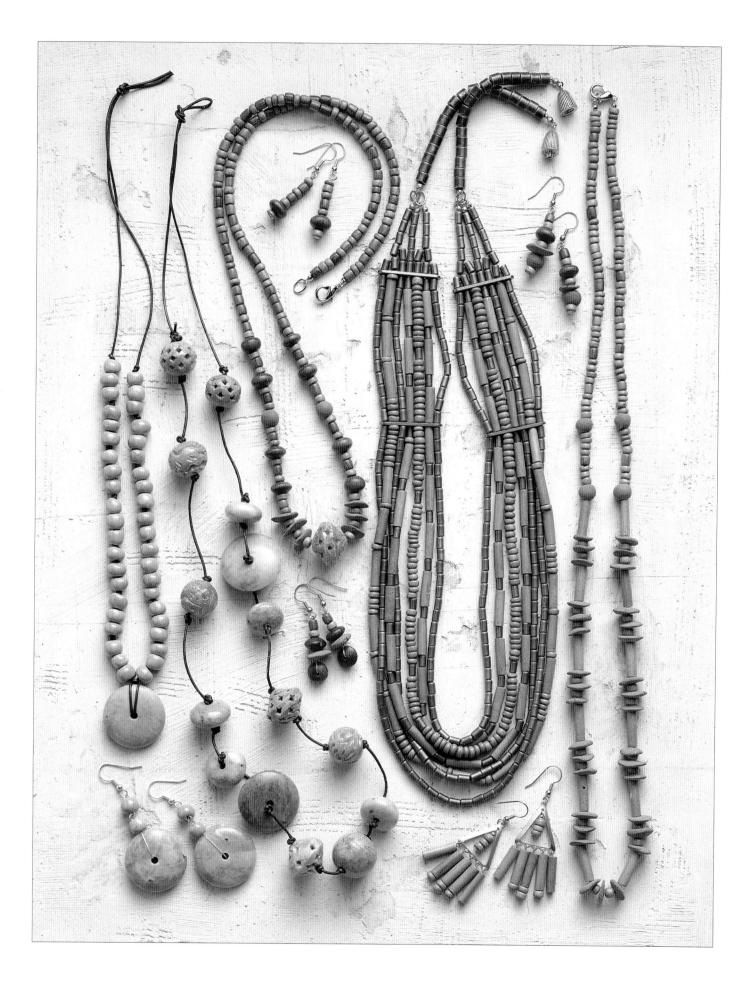

Project: *Single-strand Necklace with Shells*

1. Sort through your shells, selecting those that are more or less the same shape and size.

2. Cut a length of thread at least 1 yard (1 meter) long, thread your needle and double the thread, levelling the two ends. Loosely tie a large, spare bead to the end of the thread to stop beads accidentally sliding off, then begin to pick up the beads, beginning with black rocailles.

3. Space the shell pieces equally along the thread and separating them with about 3in (7.5cm) of rocailles. If the holes in the shell pieces are so large that they can pass over the rocailles, try to substitute the shells with ones with smaller holes. Finish by unfastening the large stopping bead. Tie a reef knot, using your needle to manoeuvre the knot as close to the beads as you can manage. Add a spot of glue, then thread back the loose ends in opposite directions under a few rocailles. Trim off the ends and if you can, hide the knot by pushing it under a bead.

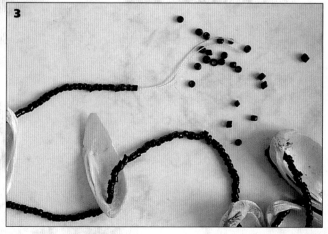

SINGLE-STRAND NECKLACE WITH SHELLS

Nothing could be simpler to make than this striking necklace. These shell fragments have a pleasing irregularity of shape, and the pretty iridescence of the inner side contrasts with the roughly textured outer side. If you have a small hobby drill, you could use shells you find on the seashore – fit a fine bit to your drill and, if necessary, increase the size of the hole by working it with a needle file. Using shells you find yourself could, in fact, be a better option, because bought ready-drilled shells tend to have irregularly placed holes. You could use similar pieces of shell to make matching earrings.

You will need
black rocailles
12 shell fragments
white thread
beading needle

Overleaf: These two necklace feature natural materials – shells and wood – but although they are both strung in the same basic way, they look entirely different. The wooden necklace has a simple ring and hook fastener, with the knot in the thread hidden by simple tubes. The shell necklace is sufficiently long not to need a fastener. Both materials are light enough to be strung on ordinary polyester thread.

DOUBLE LOOPS

One of the easiest ways of stringing heavy beads with small holes is to pass the thread twice through all the beads. Leaving a tail of about 2in (5cm), thread on five or six beads. Take the thread through the loop of a clasp, and then take it back through the same beads before threading on the remaining beads. Take the thread through the loop of the other half of the clasp before taking it back through the same beads. When you reach the left end, tie a neat knot, then thread the two spare ends through three or four beads – it is neater if you take each end in a different direction – before clipping the ends as close as you can. For extra security, you can add a spot of glue to the knot before sliding it under a bead.

WOODEN BEAD NECKLACE

The small beads used here are made from ramin. Ramin dowel will be familiar to anyone who has visited a do-it-yourself store, and the beads are simply lengths of dowel with a hole drilled through the center, cut to length and roughly shaped. The rather irregular, uneven finish gives a natural look to this simple necklace, which is light enough to be made with thread.

You will need
3 bicone wooden beads, 18mm
6 washers
about 72 wooden beads, 5mm
hook and ring
2 silver-plated tubes
tiger tail or thread
beading needle

Project: *Wooden Bead Necklace*

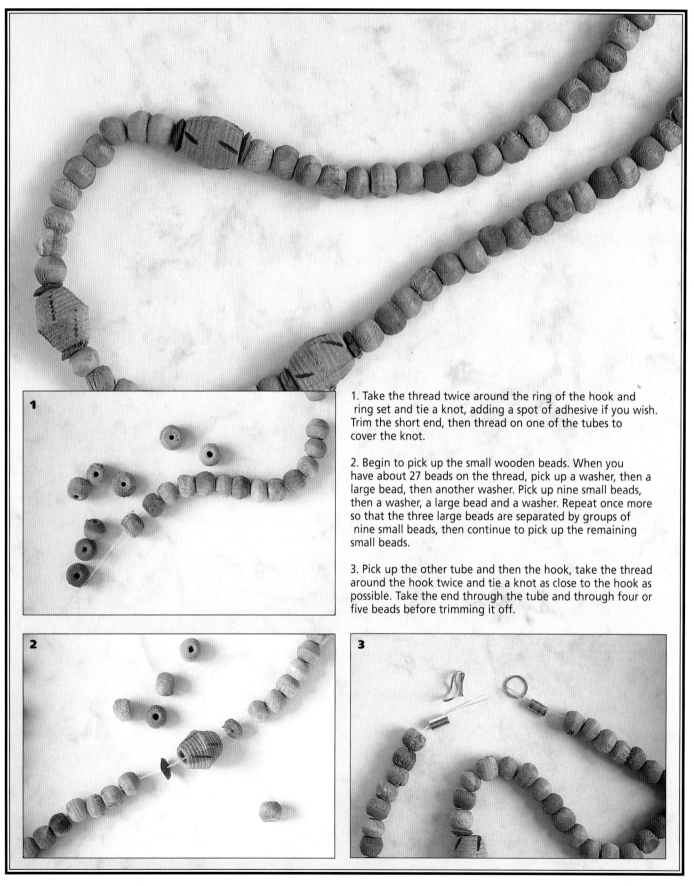

1. Take the thread twice around the ring of the hook and ring set and tie a knot, adding a spot of adhesive if you wish. Trim the short end, then thread on one of the tubes to cover the knot.

2. Begin to pick up the small wooden beads. When you have about 27 beads on the thread, pick up a washer, then a large bead, then another washer. Pick up nine small beads, then a washer, a large bead and a washer. Repeat once more so that the three large beads are separated by groups of nine small beads, then continue to pick up the remaining small beads.

3. Pick up the other tube and then the hook, take the thread around the hook twice and tie a knot as close to the hook as possible. Take the end through the tube and through four or five beads before trimming it off.

Project: *Dyed Seed Necklace*

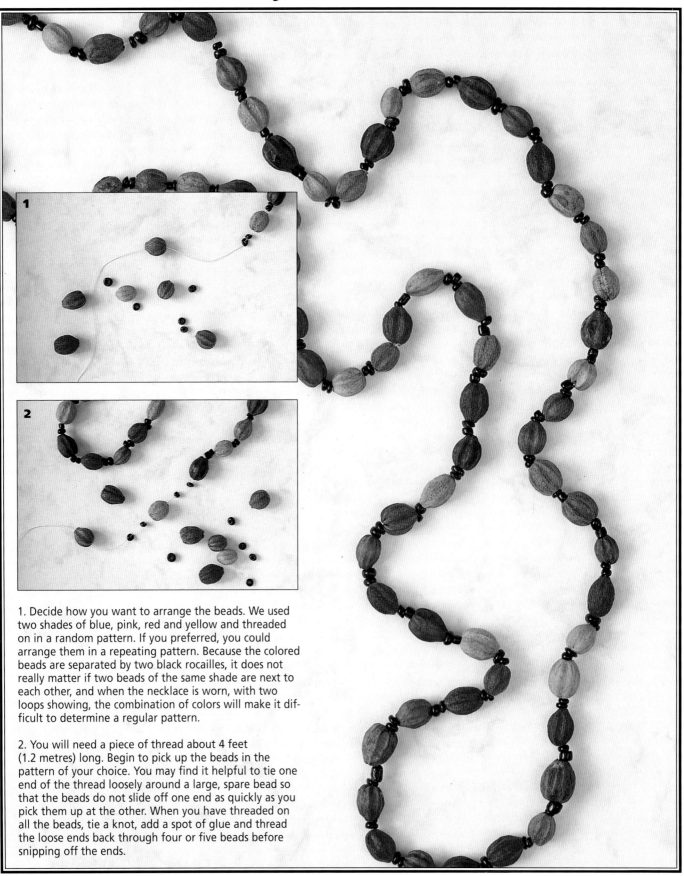

1. Decide how you want to arrange the beads. We used two shades of blue, pink, red and yellow and threaded on in a random pattern. If you preferred, you could arrange them in a repeating pattern. Because the colored beads are separated by two black rocailles, it does not really matter if two beads of the same shade are next to each other, and when the necklace is worn, with two loops showing, the combination of colors will make it difficult to determine a regular pattern.

2. You will need a piece of thread about 4 feet (1.2 metres) long. Begin to pick up the beads in the pattern of your choice. You may find it helpful to tie one end of the thread loosely around a large, spare bead so that the beads do not slide off one end as quickly as you pick them up at the other. When you have threaded on all the beads, tie a knot, add a spot of glue and thread the loose ends back through four or five beads before snipping off the ends.

DYED SEED NECKLACE

This colorful necklace is also made from natural materials – this time brightly dyed seeds – combined with black rocailles. The seeds are very light, and the holes are rather uneven. Monofilament would not be suitable, partly because the beads are not heavy enough to hold the nylon gut in a smooth curve, and partly because it would be too coarse to pass through the sometimes very small holes.

You will need
about 90 colorful beads, 10mm
black rocailles
thread
beading needle

BLUE AND SILVER SINGLE-STRAND NECKLACE

These ice blue beads make a cool, summery necklace. Interest has been added by using a few metallic beads. Again, this long string does not need a fastener, as it can be put over the head.

You will need
6 blue glass discs, 15mm
6 metal-finish beads, 3mm
128 blue glass beads, 3mm
tiger tail or thread
beading needle

Below: Pale colored glass beads always look pretty. The blue necklace is described in detail overleaf. The creamy-yellow necklace is made in the same way, with interest added by the use of different sized beads. Because these beads are translucent, use white thread.

Project: *Blue & Silver Single-strand Necklace*

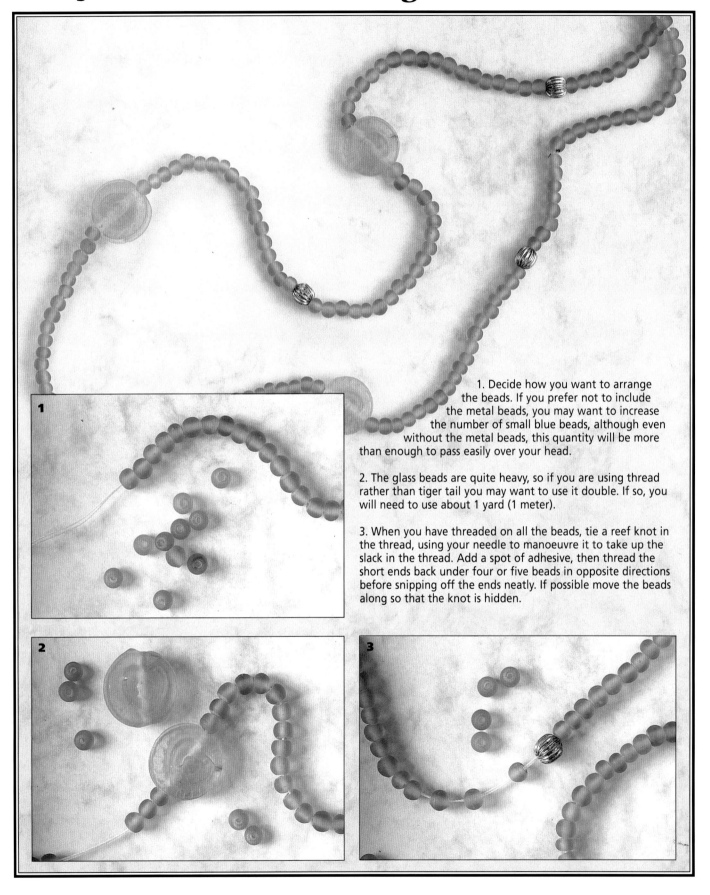

1. Decide how you want to arrange the beads. If you prefer not to include the metal beads, you may want to increase the number of small blue beads, although even without the metal beads, this quantity will be more than enough to pass easily over your head.

2. The glass beads are quite heavy, so if you are using thread rather than tiger tail you may want to use it double. If so, you will need to use about 1 yard (1 meter).

3. When you have threaded on all the beads, tie a reef knot in the thread, using your needle to manoeuvre it to take up the slack in the thread. Add a spot of adhesive, then thread the short ends back under four or five beads in opposite directions before snipping off the ends neatly. If possible move the beads along so that the knot is hidden.

COCO BEAD NECKLACE

Coco beads are available in every imaginable color. They are light and easy to thread and are, therefore, ideal for children. Although you can buy gold-colored coco beads, you can dress up ordinary wooden beads by spraying them with gold paint. Support the beads on cocktail sticks stuck in a cork or on a fine knitting needle and coat them evenly with gold spray paint. Make sure that you work in a well-ventilated room and that you protect your work surface. Part of the charm of wooden beads, even inexpensive coco beads like these, is that they are not identical, varying slightly not only in size but also in color.

Overleaf: Wooden beads can be used on their own or combined with glass and plastic to create interesting textures. The natural colors always look beautiful, especially when the grain in the wood is visible and has been enhanced by the smoothly shining surface.

You will need
9 gold-painted coco beads, 5mm
18 gold-painted coco beads, 3mm
about 225 coco beads, 3mm
monofilament

Project: *Coco Bead Necklace*

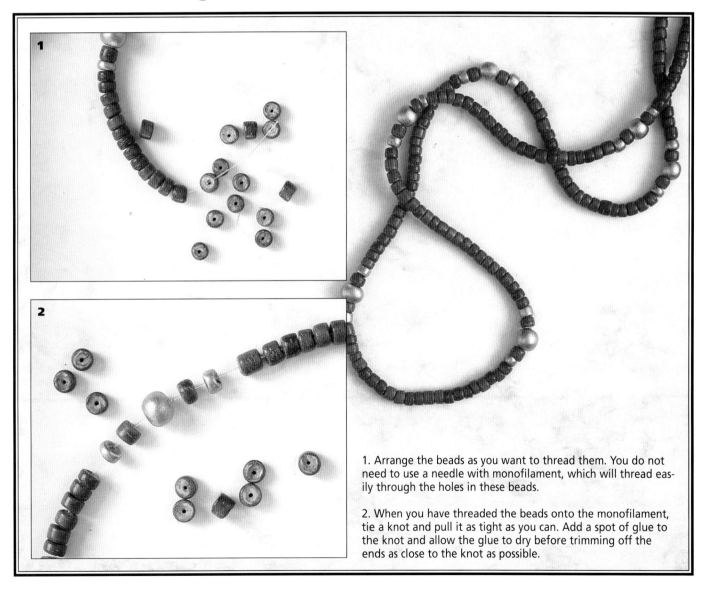

1. Arrange the beads as you want to thread them. You do not need to use a needle with monofilament, which will thread easily through the holes in these beads.

2. When you have threaded the beads onto the monofilament, tie a knot and pull it as tight as you can. Add a spot of glue to the knot and allow the glue to dry before trimming off the ends as close to the knot as possible.

Project: *Black & White Single-strand Necklace*

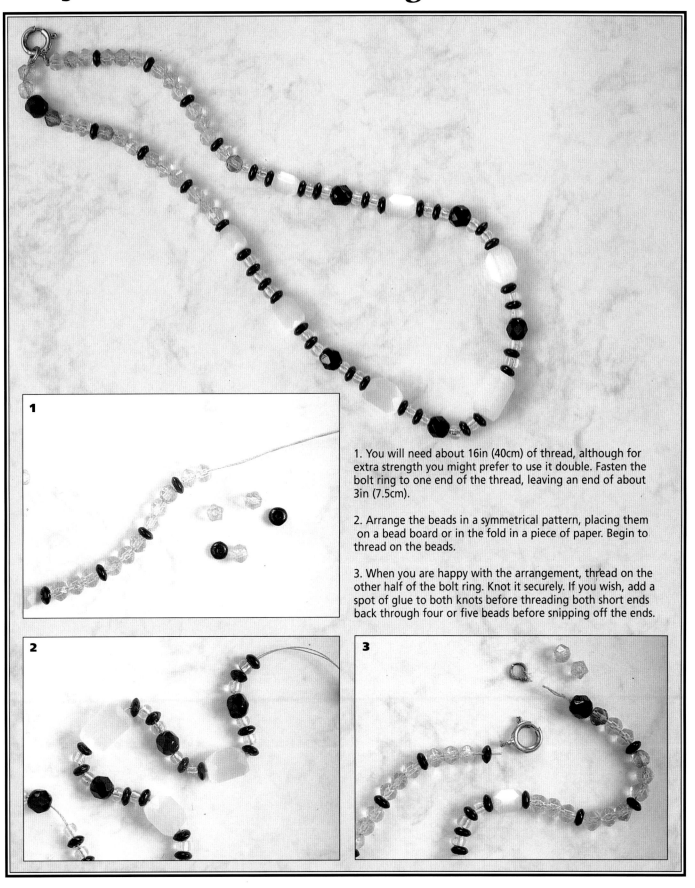

1. You will need about 16in (40cm) of thread, although for extra strength you might prefer to use it double. Fasten the bolt ring to one end of the thread, leaving an end of about 3in (7.5cm).

2. Arrange the beads in a symmetrical pattern, placing them on a bead board or in the fold in a piece of paper. Begin to thread on the beads.

3. When you are happy with the arrangement, thread on the other half of the bolt ring. Knot it securely. If you wish, add a spot of glue to both knots before threading both short ends back through four or five beads before snipping off the ends.

MAKING A CHAIN TASSEL

You can buy curb chain, which can be easily cut to lengths of about 1¼in (3cm) with wire cutters. Cut a small length of fine silver wire and thread on the lengths of chain. Tightly close the wire to form a circle, and twist the ends of the wire together, weaving them back over the closed loop of the circle to finish it neatly. You can attach the tassel to your necklace either by means of a jump ring or, if you have made a very small wire circle, by threading a bead onto a headpin and taking the shaft of the headpin through the center of the wire circle so that the circle and chain lengths rest on the bead. Trim the headpin to length, turn a loop in it and attach it to your necklace.

Previous page: Even ordinary black plastic beads can be made to look special when they are combined with small "silver" beads and a tassel. The discs can either be distributed evenly among the round beads, or they can be used to enhance the tassel by threading both working ends through five or six before finishing off with a single large bead and the tassel.

rocailles or bugles on lengths of thread, which can then be fastened together under a simple bell cap.

You will need
1 black bead, 15mm
10 black discs
about 90 black beads, 5mm
about 100 "silver" beads, 2mm
1 ready-made black tassel
beading needle and large-eyed sewing needle
thread

MULTI-STRAND NECKLACE AND TASSEL

A striking way of finishing off a multi-strand necklace made from fairly small beads like rocailles, bugles and colored glass beads is to make a tassel from the loose ends. This necklace is large enough to slip over your head, but if you wanted to attach a clasp at the back, you would have to knot the threads together and use a crimp to cover the knot before attaching the fastener. To make the necklace, thread seven strands, each about 60in (152cm) long, with a random pattern of bugles, rocailles and round glass beads, leaving about 8in (20cm) free at each end of all the strands. Follow the instructions overleaf to make the tassel.

You will need
1 round bead, about 15mm
14 round glass beads, 7mm
14 headpins
14 calotte crimps

KNOTTED NECKLACE

When expensive beads are strung, the thread is often knotted between each bead. This not only protects the beads by preventing them from rubbing against each other but also means that if the thread should break, the beads will not roll away in all directions. If you prefer, you can use beading tweezers instead of a needle to manoeuvre the bead.

You will need
thread
beads
beading needles

MULTI-STRAND WOODEN NECKLACE

When you choose the large beads for this kind of necklace, make sure that they have a large hole. These lightweight beads can be strung on fine polyester thread without danger of their weight breaking the thread. Do not string the beads too tightly or they will not fall smoothly.

You will need
18 large wooden beads, 15mm
about 1500 small wooden beads, 3mm
thread
6 beading needles

Project: *Black and Silver Single-strand Necklace with Tassel*

1. Cut a length of thread. You will need about 30in (75cm) for this quantity of beads, although for security, you might prefer to use the thread double. Allow an extra 8in (20cm) or so for attaching the tassel. Arrange the beads, with the small black and "silver" beads alternating and introducing the discs between every 16 or 17 black beads.

2. Leaving a tail of 3–4in (7.5–10cm), pick up all the small beads. Tie the ends together as close to the beads as possible, using your needle to manoeuvre the knot. Do not trim the thread.

3. (Main picture) If possible, thread both ends through the eye of an ordinary sewing needle. If you cannot do this, thread one of the ends and take it back through five or six beads before trimming it off, then work with the remaining end as for the double ends. Pick up the large bead and take the threads down through the center of the tassel. Tie a knot and add a spot of adhesive before bringing the thread back through the large bead and finishing off by threading it back through five or six beads.

Technique: *Multi-strand Necklace & Tassel*

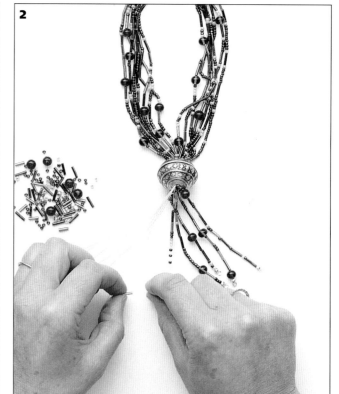

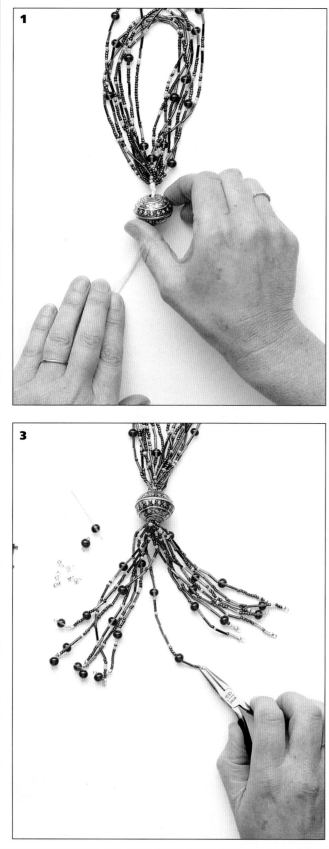

1. Knot all 14 loose ends together and thread them through the large bead.

2. Thread each end with a random pattern of beads, making each strand a different length. Finish off each strand with a knot, and squeeze a calotte crimp over the knot, with the loop on the crimp downwards.

3. Thread the 14 round beads onto headpins, clip to length and turn a loop in each pin. Attach the beads to the loops in the crimps. Alternatively, finish each strand with a rocaille or tiny bead and take the thread back up the strand to secure it.

A classic example of a simple knotted necklace, clearly demonstrating the effective combination of plain and decorated beads.

Technique: *Knotted Necklace*

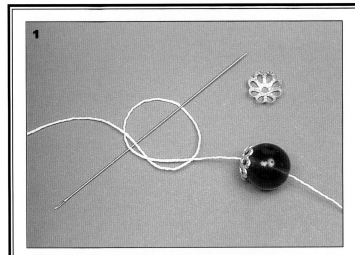

1. Tie a knot in the thread and place a needle through the loop.

2. Carefully pull the ends of the thread to tighten the knot, using the needle to manoeuvre the knot towards the bead.

3. Do not remove the needle until the knot is as close to the bead as possible. Slide the needle out of the knot and use your thumbnail to press the knot close to the bead.

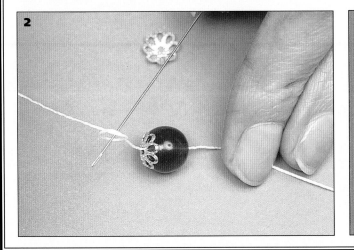

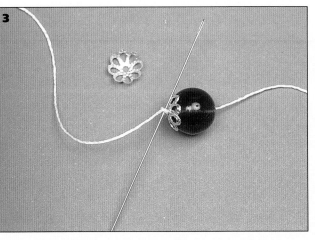

Project: *Multi-strand Wooden Necklace*

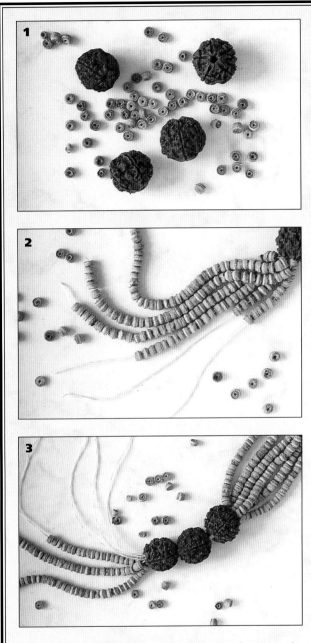

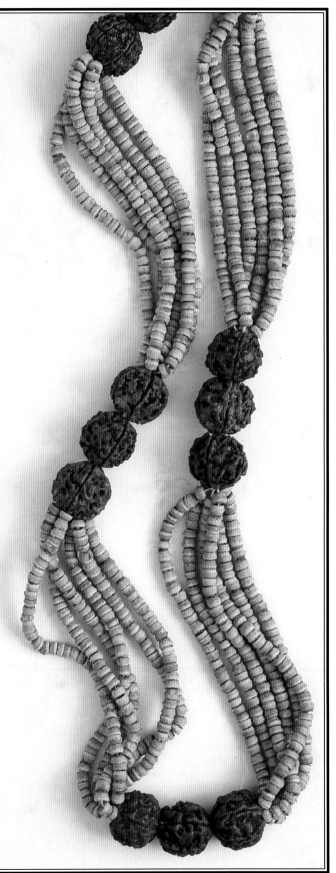

1. Decide how you want to arrange the beads. We used about 40 of the small beads between each of the large beads.

2. Cut six strands of thread, each about 1 yard (1 meter) long, and tie them together at one end. Begin by threading two of the large beads onto all six threads. Then on each thread pick up about 40 of the small beads.

3. Take all six threads through three large beads, then separate the threads to pick up further groups of 40. Continue until you pick up the last large bead, then knot the threads together to close the necklace. Add a spot of glue, trim off the ends and slide the knot under one of the large beads.

TWO-STRAND BLACK NECKLACE

Rocailles and bugles are available in a wide range of shades, so you will have no problems in finding matching colors. If you use glass beads, you will need to use tiger tail because they will be heavy. Plastic beads can be threaded on ordinary beading thread.

You will need
22 black faceted beads, 12mm
27 black faceted beads, 8mm
black bugles
black rocailles
tiger tail or thread
beading needle
calotte crimps
jump ring and bolt fastener

MULTI-STRAND CHOKER WITH SPACER BARS

Spacer bars are useful when you want to make multi-strand chokers and bracelets. These beads are all plastic but you can buy similar bone and wooden beads. The fastening here is simply two lengths of black cord, knotted through jump rings, which makes the choker suitable for any size. You could use bolt rings or a different kind of clasp if you preferred.

You will need
4 cream 3-hole spacers
6 cream tubes
3 black tubes
44 black beads, 5mm
21 "silver" beads, 3mm
18 cream beads, 3mm
thread
beading needle
calotte crimps
jump rings
black cord, about 30in (75cm)

KNOTTED CORD NECKLACE

Cord and leather thong are ideal for chunky, rather casual jewelry. We chose beige cotton cord for these wooden beads. Simply place the cords or thong inside the crimp, and use flat-nosed pliers to close one side of the crimp, then the other side. Use a jump ring to attach the loop on the crimp to the loop on your chosen fastening.

You will need
1 wooden bead, 25mm
2 wooden beads, 10mm
2 wooden beads, 8mm
2 wooden beads, 3mm
2 fluted wooden beads, 10mm
2 fluted wooden beads, 8mm
4 discs, 10mm
cord, about 4 feet (1.2 metres)

Opposite: Whether you use inexpensive black beads spaced with rocailles and bugles, or whether you use expensive crystals with a pretty clasp, the principle is the same. Make one of the strands slightly longer than the other so that they lie smoothly when the necklace is worn.

Project: *Two-strand Black Necklace*

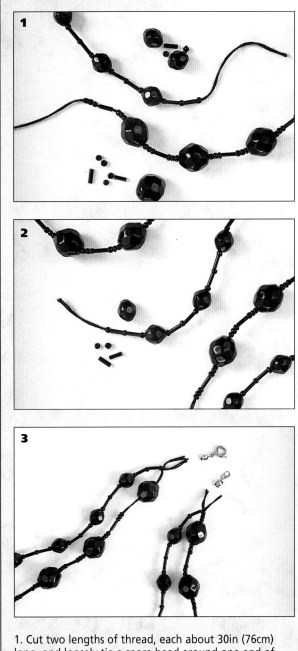

1. Cut two lengths of thread, each about 30in (76cm) long, and loosely tie a spare bead around one end of each. Begin to thread the beads on one thread, separating each of the smaller black beads with a rocaille, a bugle, a rocaille, a bugle and another rocaille.

2. Thread the other strand, separating each large bead by three rocailles, one bugle and three rocailles.

3. When you have threaded both strands, knot the ends of the strands together and add a spot of adhesive at each end. Enclose each knot within a calotte crimp and close the calottes with your pliers. Carefully open the loops on the bolt and jump ring and attach them to the calottes.

Project: *Multi-strand Choker with Spacer bars*

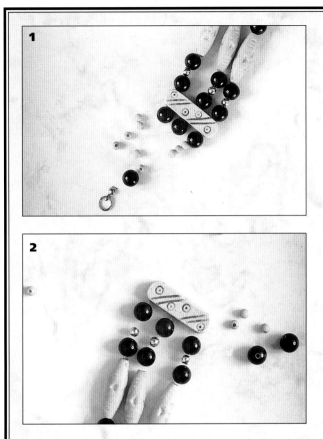

1. Cut three lengths of thread, each about 16in (40cm) long. Knot them together, add a spot of adhesive, trim the ends and enclose the knot in a calotte crimp. Use long-nosed pliers to close the crimp. Pick up one black bead on all three threads, then begin to pick up the beads in your chosen pattern. When you are working with spacer bars, you can either work one complete thread, remembering to take the first row through the top hole in the spacer bars, or you can work all the threads simultaneously, which, when the rows are the same, as in this case, helps to ensure that every row is identical. Remember, too, that spacer bars like this have a right and a wrong side, so be careful that you take the threads through the appropriate holes each time.

2. When you have threaded on all the beads, tie the threads together as close to the final bead as possible, add a spot of adhesive, trim the ends and enclose the knot in a calotte. Close the calotte crimp. Open a large jump ring and pass it through the loop of the calotte. Close the ring. Cut the cord into two equal lengths. Knot one length through the jump ring and tie the ends together, trimming them neatly. Repeat at the other end.

Above and Opposite: Simple pendants like these are easily made with a length of leather thong or lace cord, and they are the perfect showcase for one or two really beautiful beads. Choose a thong or cord that contrasts with or complements your beads.

Left: Ordinary discs make quite beautiful pendants. Combine them with smaller fluted or patterned beads to display them at their best.

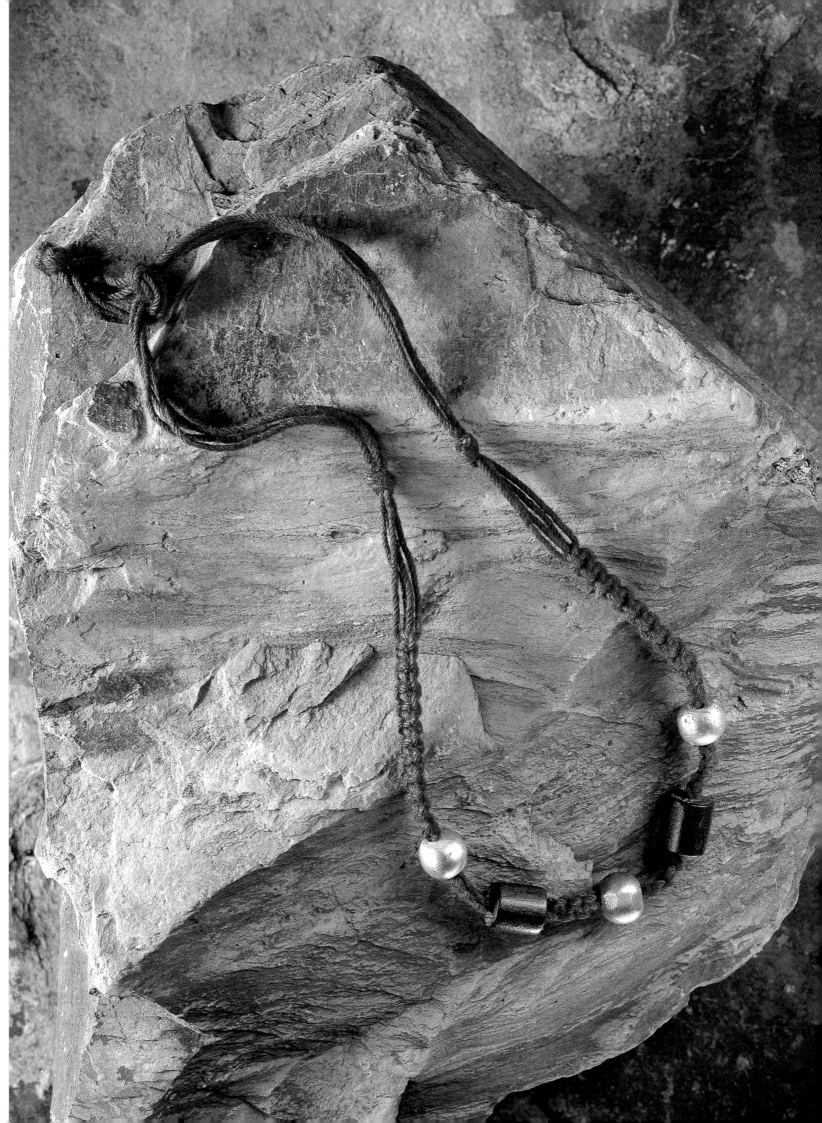

Project: *Beaded Brooch*

1. Use the thread double for extra strength. Attach the thread to the disc, then make a large loop of beads. Attach rows of single beads, then make a second, matching loop at the opposite side.

2. Make two long, single drops, holding the beads on the thread by using a small bead at the end and taking the thread up through the other beads again. Secure any loose ends on the back of the disc with spots of adhesive before attaching the back of the sieve.

CHAPTER FOUR
WIREWORK

WIREWORK

Headpins and eyepins make it possible to make the most amazing range of earrings and drop ornaments to add to necklaces. Turning smooth, even loops is not easy, and it is worth practising on lengths of wire until you are confident that you can turn a neat loop every time. Always keep some spare head and eyepins, and do not be afraid to discard any that are not perfectly straight and any that you have worked to and fro – such metal is prone to snapping.

You will find manipulating rings easier if you use two pairs of pliers. For example, when you need to bend or close a ring, hold the ring firmly in one pair of pliers and close or open it with the other pair. When you are opening a loop to add a jump ring or another loop, open the loops sideways. Never close loops by trying to squeeze the metal together. You will force the loop or ring out of shape and probably weaken the metal.

Opposite: With just a few head or eyepins, some pliers and a few pretty beads you can make some stunning earrings.

Below: Wooden beads, faux pearls and pretty little plastic flowers are ideal for drop earrings. If you use simple fish hook ear fittings, you can slip different drops and loops on and off the same hook.

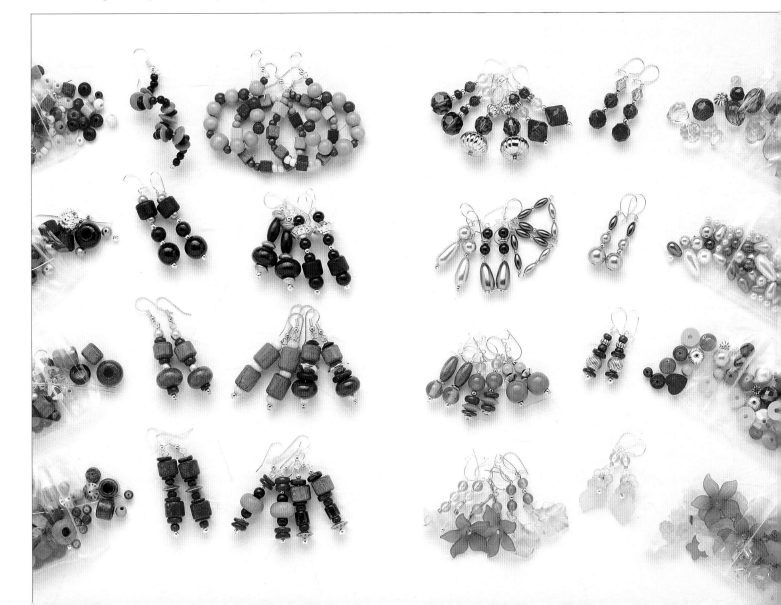

Opposite: Your earrings can be as simple or as complicated as you wish, and there is such a wide range of pretty drop beads available that it is difficult to know what to choose. The simplest kind of kidney ear wires can, in fact, be used with a variety of drop arrangements, because the top loop of the arrangement or chain simply slides into place on the ear wire.

SIMPLE DROP EARRINGS

You could hardly find easier earrings to make. This style is the perfect introduction to using your metal snips and round-nosed pliers. Use whatever long bead you wish – look out for Peruvian ceramic beads, which are available in attractive shades of warm ocher and rich brown as well as blues and greens.

You will need
2 drop beads, about 20mm
2 beads, about 5mm
6 tiny beads
2 long headpins
1 pair of ear wires

Techniques: *Simple Drop Earrings*

1. Thread the beads onto the headpins, beginning with a tiny bead to prevent the other beads from falling off the bottom .

3. Turn a neat loop in the top of each headpin with your round-nosed pliers, slip on an ear wire and close the loop.

2. Trim each headpin so that it is about 1/4in (6mm) longer than the beads.

CHAPTER FIVE

WEAVING &
LOOMWORK

Weaving & Loomwork

Although simply strung beads offer almost limitless opportunities for creating unusual necklaces, other simple techniques can be used to introduce variety of form and texture into your beadwork. Free-hand weaving offers scope for some exceptionally elegant necklaces and bracelets, while loomwork is traditionally associated with North American bead work.

Techniques: *Two Threads*

1. Thread a long piece of thread – you will need about 27in (69cm) for a necklace – on each needle. Pick up a bead on each needle.

2. Push the beads down the threads so that they are level.

3. Pick up a single bead on the left-hand needle, and take the right-hand needle through the bead in the opposite direction.

4. Push the bead down so that it sits evenly between the two earlier beads, then pick up a bead on each needle and begin again.

WEAVING

Wonderfully elegant chokers of crystal or jet of the type that were so popular in Edwardian England, or colorful bracelets of tiny opaque rocailles are not difficult to make. Make sure that the beads you use are the same size and that the holes run through the center. This is especially important if you are using faceted beads. The first sequence shows how a simple pattern – apparently of three rows, but worked with two threads – can be built up. The second uses a single thread to produce a repeating hexagonal pattern of beads.

Below: The techniques used here are almost infinitely adaptable. For example, it would be possible to use a tube as the central bead through which both threads are carried, with three or four beads picked up on the single threads to form the border.

TWO THREADS

This technique is ideal for chokers – crystals look especially good when they are worked in this way. Because you are working with two threads, a two-strand diamanté clasp is a suitable way of beginning and ending the necklace.

You will need
beads
beading thread
2 beading needles

Techniques: *Multi Threads*

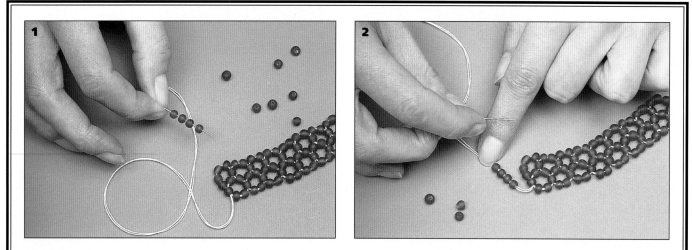

1. Using a double length of thread, pick up six beads. Tie the thread in a knot to form a circle of beads. Take the thread back through two beads and pick up five beads, miss one bead and take the thread through the next bead on the circle of six you began with. Pick up four beads.

2. Push these four beads down the thread. You will find it easier to work on a flat surface rather than allowing the beads to hang from your hand, especially as your work gets longer and heavier.

3. Miss the first bead in the preceding circle and take your needle through the next bead. In each circle, you have the four beads you have just picked up, and a bead from each of the two preceding circles, forming a hexagonal pattern.

4. Carefully draw the thread through the needle, tightening it carefully to close the circle but being careful that you do not pull it so taut that the bead circles are distorted.

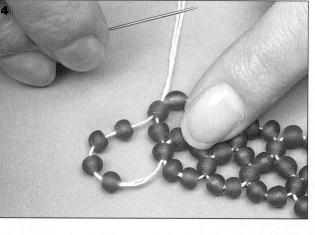

Techniques: *Loom Work*

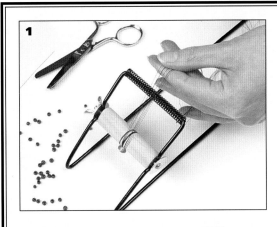

1. Cut each thread 18–20in (46–51cm) longer than the length of your finished piece. Knot the ends together and arrange the threads over the loom so that there is an even length of spare thread at each end. Attach one knot to the protruding pin in the roll or tube of your loom and wind the spare threads around the cylinder to keep them out the way.

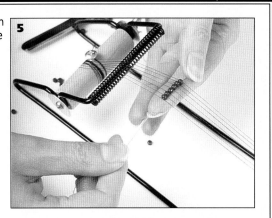

2. Use a needle or something similar to separate the threads so that each one passes through one of the grooves in the spring.

3. Taking care to keep the threads straight and separate, take them around the pin at the other end of the loom. Use your needle to make sure that each thread is separate and straight before winding the spare thread onto the cylinder at the other end.

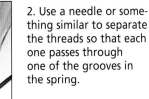

4. Take a new length of thread – this will be the weft thread – and, using a beading needle, pick up the appropriate number of beads. Run the beads towards the end of the thread, leaving a tail of about 3in (7.5cm). Hold the beads under the warp threads and push them up so that each bead lies in the space between the warp threads. The weft thread lies under the warp threads.

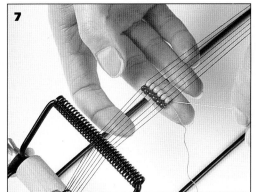

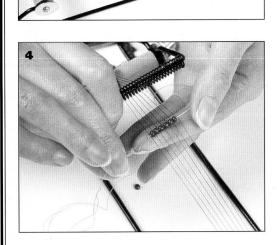

5. Now, thread your needle through the beads, but take the working thread over all the warp threads – that is, the weft thread passes twice through each bead, with the warp threads held between it. Try it. It does work.

6. Pull your needle through so that the weft threads are taut and tie the working end and your tail together. When you have worked several rows, the tail end can be taken back through several beads and snipped off.

7. Pick up your next row of beads and repeat the process, making sure that you push each row that you complete right up against the previous row.

Opposite: Rocailles tend to vary slightly in shape, and the holes do not always go precisely through the center. These slight irregularities can be charming, but when you are working a geometric pattern on a loom, it is worth discarding any beads that are grossly misshapen because they will distort your work and make your pattern look uneven.

Below: Although looms are often used to work striking geometric patterns, single colored rocailles can be used with surprising results, and the iridescent rocailles have created a subtly shaded bracelet.

MULTI THREADS

Because the finished effect is decorative in its own right, patterned beads are rather wasted with this technique, but you could use textured metal beads, for example, instead of the plain ground glass beads we have used. Leave a fairly long thread when you begin, and use it to make a loop of, say, matching rocailles. When you have finished, use the working thread to pick up several rocailles, a large bead and, if you wish, more rocailles and a further large bead, which can be used as a fastening for the necklace or bracelet.

You will need
beads
beading needle
thread

LOOMWORK

Loomwork is immediately evocative of Native American crafts, and a loom is often used to make belts and hatbands in the distinctive patterns and colors of this style. However, looms can be used for smaller items, including pieces that are attached to earrings and brooches, and it is the ideal way of making a narrow, elegant choker. You might even want to experiment by weaving names or pictorial motifs, or to stitch several pieces together

Looms are easy to use as long as you follow a few basic rules. The most important of these is that when you are laying the threads that run the length of the work, the warp threads, you must have one more thread than the number of beads across your design – thus, if your design is eight beads wide, you will need nine threads and so on.

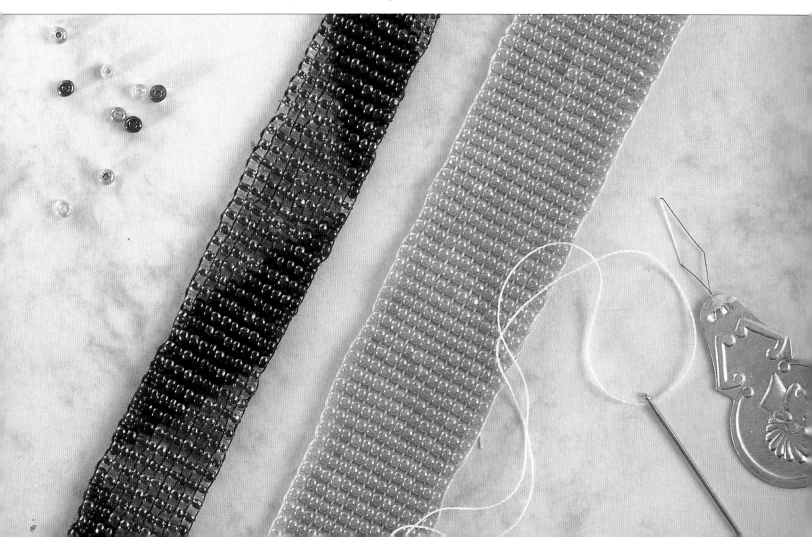

EMBROIDERY

Opposite: Rocailles and bugles used to be sold by length, ready threaded, rather than by weight, and when you are using them to decorate fabric, this is convenient because you can couch down the thread, rather than attach individual beads.

Translucent gold-colored rocailles have been stitched onto this black velvet stole to create an elegant and eye-catching accessory for an evening dress.

Anyone who has ever done any needlework will have pieces of even-weave fabric left over, and stitching patterns and even pictorial designs with small and medium sized rocailles seems to have taken over from cross stitch as the favorite handicraft at the moment. Bugles and rocailles can be used to decorate all kinds of objects, from small greetings cards to underwear.

Sequins are often used with rocailles, and the iridescent or pearlized rocailles look very pretty with glinting sequins, which can be held in place by bringing the thread up through the hole, picking up a rocaille and taking the thread back through the hole, so that the rocaille anchors the sequin.

If you have the patience, you could use opaque rocailles to work a picture like the one on this antique footstool.

PURPLE WAISTCOAT

Beads don't have to be used only on items of jewelry. Bugles and rocailles are particularly useful if you want to brighten up a plain handbag, but why not thread some beads onto fine elastic to make a useful spectacle cord, or stitch some bright beads in a random pattern on a colorful headband? You can even decorate a pair of socks!

You will need
about 2 yards (2 meters) of different colored cord
assorted beads, including rocailles and flat discs
tailor's chalk (optional)
dressmaking pins
needle
sewing thread to match

Above and left: Little shell beads and pink "pearls" have been stitched around the edge of this pincushion. This is an easy and unusual way to decorate something as small as a pincushion or as large as a full-size cushion.

117

Project: *Purple Waistcoat*

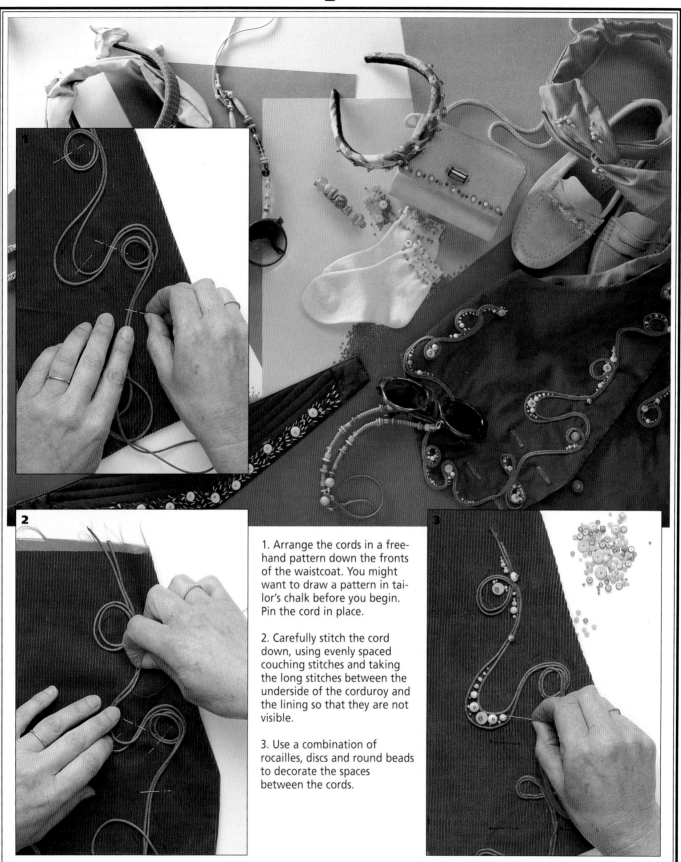

1. Arrange the cords in a free-hand pattern down the fronts of the waistcoat. You might want to draw a pattern in tailor's chalk before you begin. Pin the cord in place.

2. Carefully stitch the cord down, using evenly spaced couching stitches and taking the long stitches between the underside of the corduroy and the lining so that they are not visible.

3. Use a combination of rocailles, discs and round beads to decorate the spaces between the cords.

Techniques: *Green Jacket*

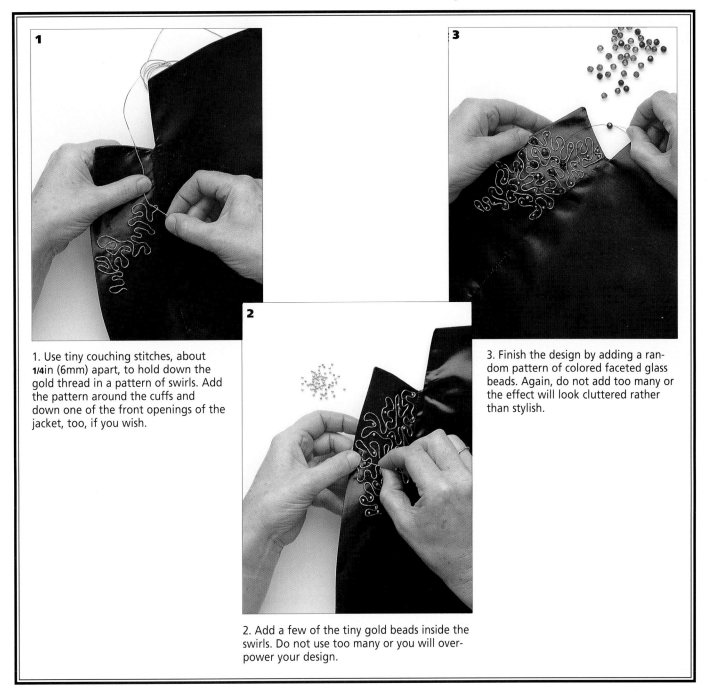

1. Use tiny couching stitches, about **1/4**in (6mm) apart, to hold down the gold thread in a pattern of swirls. Add the pattern around the cuffs and down one of the front openings of the jacket, too, if you wish.

2. Add a few of the tiny gold beads inside the swirls. Do not use too many or you will overpower your design.

3. Finish the design by adding a random pattern of colored faceted glass beads. Again, do not add too many or the effect will look cluttered rather than stylish.

GREEN JACKET

Although gold elasticated thread is useful for making simple bracelets and necklaces, it can be used as a decorative element in its own right, as seen on the lapel of this green evening jacket.

You will need
gold elastic thread
needle and invisible thread
tiny gold beads
small faceted beads

Techniques: *Blue Belt*

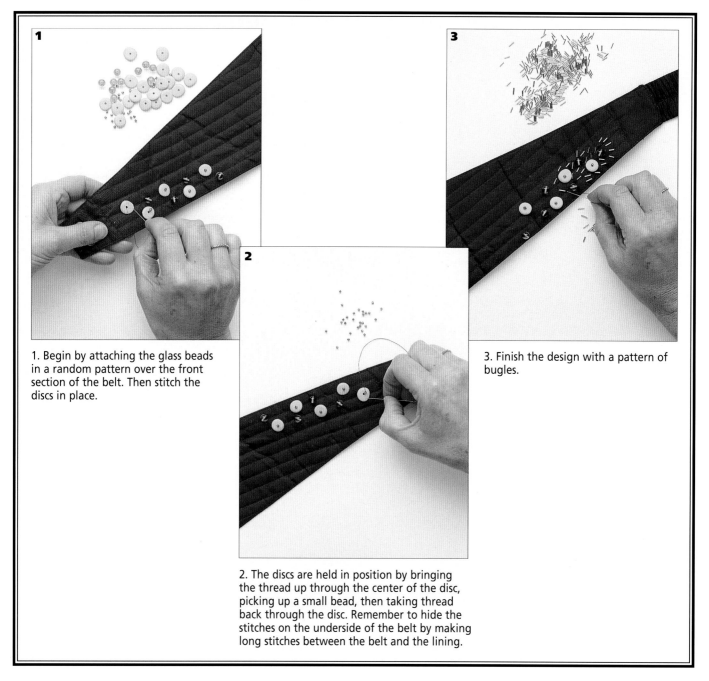

1. Begin by attaching the glass beads in a random pattern over the front section of the belt. Then stitch the discs in place.

2. The discs are held in position by bringing the thread up through the center of the disc, picking up a small bead, then taking thread back through the disc. Remember to hide the stitches on the underside of the belt by making long stitches between the belt and the lining.

3. Finish the design with a pattern of bugles.

BLUE BELT

A plain outfit can be transformed by the addition of bead-decorated accessories. Handbags are obvious candidates for adornment, but the technique can be used with equal success on a plain belt or cummerbund.

You will need
round glass beads, 7mm
discs
bugles
rocailles
needle and thread

Opposite: Keyrings can be enlivened with various elements to cheer up otherwise mundane, practical objects.

GEMSTONES

Although these are not really beads, gemstones add a new dimension to jewelry making without requiring the use of all the additional technical equipment and impedimenta that metal work or enamelling involves. Bead suppliers often also supply cabochons in a range of sizes and shapes and in the most wonderful range of stones. Combine these with the standard blanks for brooches, cuff links and so on that are so widely available to produce some unusual and personal items.

Project: *Elephant Keyring*

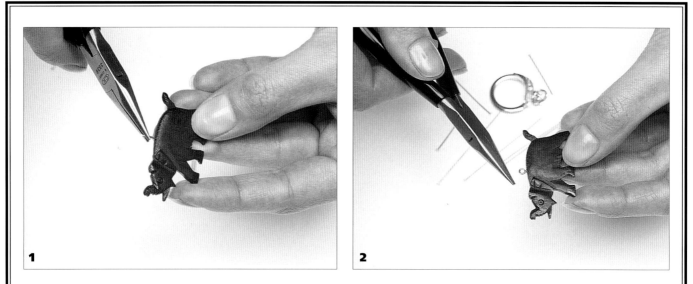

1. Insert a headpin through the elephant's body, trim it with your wire cutters to about **1/4**in (6mm) longer than the elephant.

2. Turn a loop in the top of the headpin, remembering to make sure that it is large enough to accommodate the jump ring or loop on your key chain.

3. If your key chain does not have a jump ring already attached, open a jump ring or, for extra strength, a split ring.

4. Insert the jump ring through the loop at the top of the headpin and, if necessary, through the loop at the base of the key chain. Close the ring carefully with your pliers.

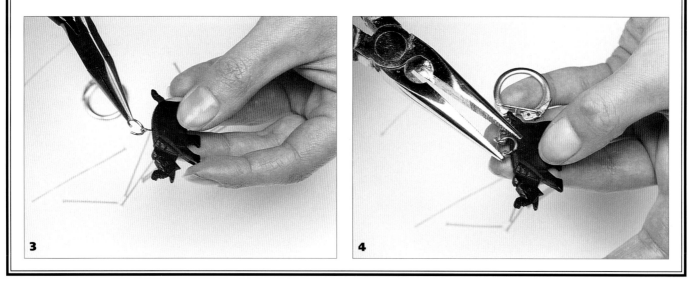

ELEPHANT KEY RING

Blank key rings, both nickel-plated and gold-plated, are widely available, and you can use all kinds of beads and bead-related items to personalize them. This little wooden elephant, for example, is one of a pair that would look equally at home on a pair of long, dangling earrings.

You will need
headpin
key chain
jump ring (optional)

TEDDY KEY RING

The little silver-plated teddy attached to this key chain has an integral loop between the ears, so it can be attached directly to a jump ring or key chain. The teddy was actually intended for use as a pendant, but it could be attached to a chain bracelet instead, and if you wanted, you could add an oval cabochon stone to his tummy.

DRAGONFLY BROOCH

Cabochon stones can be easily inserted into a variety of brooches and pendants to personalize your designs. The little dragonfly is sterling silver, but there are all kinds of insects, birds, animals and flowers to choose from. Cabochons are available ready polished in a range of sizes and stone types. If you are working with several stones, mix a two-part epoxy resin; if you are working with a single stone, a contact adhesive is a far more economical way of working.

You will need
brooch or pendant blank
cabochon, 4mm
contact adhesive or two-part epoxy resin

Techniques: *Dragonfly Brooch*

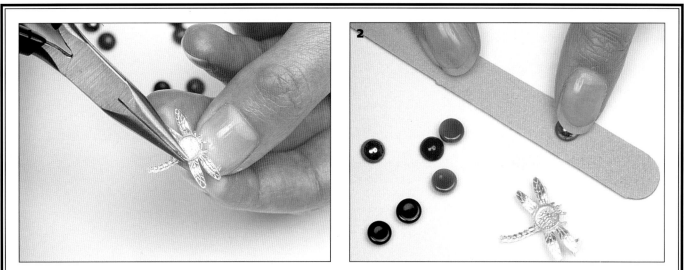

1. If necessary, use your long-nosed pliers to open slightly the lip of the aperture so that the stone will slip easily into place.

2. It is sometimes helpful to abrade the underside of a stone to improve its adhesion.

3. Apply the tiniest spot of contact adhesive to the aperture.

4. Use tweezers to position the stone, leave the adhesive to dry, then gently press back the lip around the stone to ensure that the stone will not fall out.

CHAIN BRACELET
Undrilled tumble-polished gemstones are often attached to bracelets or earrings by means of caps with loops at the top. Chains can be bought and trimmed to length and an appropriate fastenings attached, or you can obtain chains that are ready fitted with clasps or fastenings.

You will need
bracelet chain
gemstones
bell caps
jump rings
contact adhesive

Techniques: *Chain Bracelet*

1. Make sure that the gemstones are perfectly clean by wiping them with acetone or nail-varnish remover. Use a spot of contact adhesive to attach a bell cap to the end of each stone.

2. Open a jump ring sideways and use it to attach the bell caps and gemstones to the chain.

3. Space the gemstones evenly around the bracelet, and check that the points of the bell caps are firmly pressed down against the stones so that they do not catch on your clothes and weaken the join.

HAT PINS

You can buy gold and silver-finish hat and lapel pins to decorate with beads that will match your outfit.

Often, the combination of one large, very decorative bead, such as a pretty goldstone drop or a Chinese porcelain bead, with a traditional enamel and gilded pattern, with a few plain metal beads is most effective and successful.

The pins range in length from about 3¼in (8cm) to over 5in (13cm), and they are used with little caps, which cover the points. Most pins are in the style of an ordinary headpin – that is, they have a small flat knob at the top end. If you place a small plain bead on first, the other, larger beads will not be able to fall off.

Overleaf: Lapel and hat pins are a good way of using single, attractive beads. Here are just a few suggestions, ranging from hand-painted ceramic beads from Peru to natural wooden beads.